HOMELAND SECURITY
ATE MY SPEECH

ARIEL DORFMAN

HOMELAND SECURITY ATE MY SPEECH

Messages From the End of the World

WITHDRAWN

O/R

OR BOOKS
NEW YORK • LONDON

© Ariel Dorfman

All rights information: rights@orbooks.com
Visit our website at www.orbooks.com

First printing 2017

Library of Congress Cataloging-in-Publication Data: A catalog
record for this book is available from the Library of Congress.

British Library Cataloging in Publication Data: A catalog
record for this book is available from the British Library.

Interior Design by Pauline Neuwirth

Published for the book trade by OR Books in partnership
with Counterpoint Press.

Distributed to the trade by Publishers Group West.

paperback ISBN 978-194486-963-2
ebook ISBN 978-194486-964-9

This book, as always, is for Angélica,
who has kept me sane in the insane America
that has created Donald Trump.

CONTENTS

INTRODUCTION: Grieving For America   1

PART ONE

THE RISE OF DONALD J. TRUMP

1. Phillip II, the Sixteenth Century Spanish Monarch, Writes to His Excellency Donald Trump   13

2. America Meets Frankenstein   17

3. My Mother and Trump's Border   23

4. Latin American Food and the Failure of Trump's Wall   29

5. Faulkner's Question for America   37

PART TWO

THE JUDGMENT OF HISTORY

6. Now, America, You Know How Chile Felt   45

7. The River Kwai Passes Through the Latin America and the Potomac: What it Feels Like to be Tortured   51

8. Words of Encouragement for Donald J. Trump from James Buchanan, the 15th President of the United States   59

9. A Message from the End of the World   65

10. Should Iago Be Tortured?   69

11. Mission Akkomplished: From Comrade
     Bush to Tovarisch Trump   75

PART THREE

MODELS OF RESISTANCE FROM THE PAST

12. Martin Luther King Marches On   87

13. Searching for Mandela   95

14. The Truth That Made Her Free   117

15. Reading Cervantes in Captivity   123

16. The Dancing Cosmos of Albert Einstein   131

17. Revisiting Melville in Chile   135

PART FOUR

WHAT IS TO BE DONE?

18. Homeland Security Ate My Speech   155

19. Alice in Leftland: Will You, Won't You Dance?   175

20. They're Watching Us: So What?   183

21. How We Overcame Tyranny Before: Take Heart, Friends   197

22. The Whispering Leaves of the Hiroshima Ginko Trees   203

A NOTE ON THE ESSAYS   207

ACKNOWLEDGEMENTS   211

HOMELAND SECURITY
ATE MY SPEECH

INTRODUCTION

GRIEVING FOR AMERICA

O N November 9th, 2016, the day after the election of *Donald J. Trump as President of the United States, I wrote an anguished meditation that, now, as I prepare to publish the articles and essays I composed during his astounding rise to power, seems to be the perfect prologue to this book.*

Here is what I wrote:

I can no longer deny it.

I feel that, by electing an ignorant, belligerent misogynist, a race-baiting, Mexican-hating predator, a liar who does not believe in climate change and who will increase the affliction of the neediest inhabitants of his country and the world, America has revealed its true identity.

Like so many citizens of this land and so many others around the world, I am stupefied, astonished, sickened.

And yet, looking into the mirror and mirage of my life, I should not feel surprised at this apocalyptic reckoning.

When my wife Angélica and I brought our family to the United States in 1980, we had no illusions about what sort of nation greeted us. We had been wandering in exile since 1973, when an American-sponsored coup in Chile against the democratically-elected President Salvador Allende installed a brutal dictatorship. We were aware, coming from what was then called the Third World, of the way in which the United States, its corporations, its military, indeed its public, were complicit in crimes against humanity on every continent. Nor were we blind to how minorities and the poor were treated in the "land of the free," or its long history of slavery and Jim Crow, its conquest of Native Americans, its maltreatment of dissidents and foreigners.

Even so, I had many reasons to thank and admire America. My Argentine family had found refuge here once before, in 1945. As a child growing up in the wondrous, blossoming city of New York, I had fallen in love with this country, a country that gave me the language in which I write this requiem for America, the music and literature that nurture me, the extraordinary experiment in search of a more perfect union, a history of resistance to prejudice and racism among its most enlightened citizens and workers. I was seduced by the generosity of a people that was able to welcome numerous immigrant communities, to boundlessly expand its multicultural explorations, and to accept so many religious groups free to practice their beliefs. A land that belonged to you and me and was constantly willing to question its own limitations. The land of Dylan and Franklin Delano Roosevelt, Meryl Streep and Walt Whitman, Ella Fitzgerald and Edgar Allan Poe. The land of Frederick Douglass. How could one not be entranced by this pursuit of happiness?

I have spent most of my hybrid, double life trying to reconcile these two Americas—one that fiercely represses our humanity and the other that gloriously expresses the best in us, a reconciliation that was made possible by the ongoing wager and prophecy that the America of the better angels that my hero Lincoln invoked would eventually prevail.

My belief in the redemption of a country where I ended up becoming a citizen, along with Angélica and our two sons, would be grievously tested over and over in the 36 years since we arrived here.

It was a schizophrenic process.

Dreadful things kept happening: the mean-spirited Reagan era of greed; the unrelenting interventions in sovereign nations culminating with the younger Bush's war-mongering; the malignant growth of the national security state; Democrats far too often subservient to money and privilege and military might. But through it all—and so much more that was disappointing and objectionable—I tried to keep faith in America, resolutely holding on to any sign that allowed me to celebrate its communal story. I searched out every encouraging mark of progress, every small act of decency and defiance by countless citizens that prefigured a country of tolerance and fairness and grace, proof that the courage and solidarity of ordinary people and extraordinary organizations formed the bedrock of the real nation.

It is this delicate balancing act that has been so tested and decentered by the rise of Trump and more fatally by the vast amount of my fellow citizens who enabled—in the worse sense of the word—his victory, which was proclaimed, by one of those chilling coincidences that history seems to love, in the early hours of this November 9th, the anniversary of Kristallnacht.

I do not wish to demonize the future President's followers. In fact, I have on various occasions written sympathetically about their quandary, grasping at the roots of their anger and bafflement, their sense of displacement, without condoning the more extreme manifestations of bigotry and hatred that animates, alas, a considerable contingent of his zealots.

But I realize now that this understanding of the causes of their disarray, that sympathy for their identity crisis, was only imaginable because I thought that Trump could not conceivably win. Now, however, that we must fully live what is inconceivable, now that this frightening man has opened a door through which everything horrible and spiteful in America has come crawling out, I cannot help but contemplate, staring back at me from the abyss of his triumph, the true face of America, the deep face, the permanent dreadful face of America, the irrevocable part of America that has always been there and that I can no longer delude myself will ever be redeemed. The suspicion that after this loathing-filled campaign and what now looms forebodingly ahead, it may be impossible to repair the rift in the community that I belong to and cannot escape.

How to continue onwards, bearing the broken heart of my identity and this poison that contaminates that identity and the whole nation, how to accept what so many innocent people are about to suffer?

I have tried to console myself with words that were gifted to me just yesterday, the day of the election, by Rasheed, an African-American man with whom I talked while, with my son Rodrigo and my granddaughters Isabella and Catalina, we canvassed neighborhoods in Durham, North Carolina, seeking out anybody who had not yet voted. This radiant man, who exuded an almost magical air of tranquility and goodness, one of those human beings who has not let himself be infected by the misfortunes that fate and the color of his skin have dealt him, recognized my alarm at the very thought that Trump might succeed.

"You just have to keep the faith," he said. "We make mistakes, but our people, in general, in the big things, in the long run, we get it right."

Noble and wise words that linger but cannot alleviate my immeasurable distress.

I began this sad rumination by writing that I felt stupefied, astonished, sickened.

All of that, yes, but something more, something much deeper and enduring.

Grief: that is what I really feel. Grief and mourning for a country that, for me and perhaps for many others, has just died, that signed its own death warrant when its citizens, the blind citizens of my land, chose Donald Trump as the man who will lead us all to devastation.

And yet, Rasheed is still there. With all the resistance, past and future, that his words and dignity and incessant promise of resurrection embody.

He will not be alone as he confronts the terror of what is to come.

The struggle has never ceased. The struggle has just begun.

May the fields of grief be full of miracles.

And that is how, with a phrase that recognized my sorrow and suggested some slim intimation of hope, I finished my November 9th contemplation of our ruined nation.

It was the culmination of a series of reflections on Donald Trump that I had penned before the election and which would be followed by many more in the next months.

Before Trump had declared his intention to seek the Presidency, he had hardly registered on the radar of my mind. I had never watched reality TV shows, didn't know the difference between *The Apprentice* and *The Sorcerer's Apprentice*, couldn't have cared less for the gossip columns or the scandals soiling the tabloid news. Two actions of that celebrity billionaire had vaguely suggested his reprehensible existence: his attempt, through false birther claims, to paint Obama as alien to America, and his campaign and full page ads demanding that five black and Latino teenagers be executed for a crime in Central Park that they had not committed.

And then he descended on his escalator from Hell to announce he was seeking the Presidency and I became very quickly obsessed with him, in a manner I am forced to recognize now as masochistic, almost perverse, and which nevertheless forced me to come to grips with his startling sway over immense swaths of the public and, regrettably, the electorate.

Like most observers, I immediately dismissed the possibility that his outlandish attempt to become the most powerful man on the planet had the slightest chance of attaining its goal. If I paid any heed at all, it was out of sick curiosity. I felt like a spectator at a circus watching an overweight clown treading on a high wire way up in the air, wondering when that performer, in this case, a racist bully, would crash spectacularly to the ground, after which he would presumably try to get up and limp away, only to slip on the banana peel of reality.

Angélica, my wife and companion for over half a century, had warned me not to be too amused or complacent. Indeed, she had announced, as soon as she saw Trump's first rally, that the coarse real estate dealer would capture the Republican nomination and then the Presidency. "He represents America," she said. "You just don't know the country if you think he won't be elected." Though I have confirmed, on innumerable occasions, that Angélica is far wiser and discerning than I could possibly ever be, I let myself scoff at her predictions.

And yet, as his campaign became ever more outrageous and anti-immigrant, more boorish and dreadful, I found myself drawn to Trump's mendacious image and his ever-contradictory statements, sucked into the vortex of the persona he was projecting. And I began, as if possessed by a demon, to write about him, at first tentatively, somewhat in jest, with unhidden contempt, and then with mounting deliberation, puzzled by the populist plutocrat's success and unnerved by at what that success portended, even if he did not win the election. And, of course, my excessive pursuit of the meaning of Trump grew proportionately as his fortunes flourished and then turned into a veritable vertigo when, after obtaining a slim electoral college majority, he seized the White House and started us all on a road to doom.

By expressing my views in a frenetic flurry of meditations, portents, exhortations, and analyses, some humorous, some deadly serious, I was not that different from countless others who, here in the States and abroad, fueled by compassion for Trump's future victims, mystified by his conservative fanatics, concerned about the future of the earth, churned out a plethora of opinions destined to fade into the dustbin of history and oblivion.

Why then did I decide to save these texts of mine from the ephemeral journalism into which they were born and collect them in this volume? As America engages in a debate about both the Meaning of Trump and the urgent question of how to block him from irreparably damaging the republic and the planet, is there anything that I can contribute?

Readers must be the ultimate judges of that, but I do believe that unless we analyze how our dire predicament came about, unless we think ourselves out of the crisis, as I have implied in one the essays in this collection, we are doomed, like Sisyphus, to keep rolling the same boulder up the hill of history, only to find ourselves one more time at the bottom, confronted with the same task.

With one difference: this time we may not get another chance.

These messages are not only written from the perspective of a country I carry inside me, the Chile that is geographically at the end of the world, but messages that also are from the end of the world in another sense, as I am haunted by the fear that the end of our humanity is closer than ever before, that our species could in a matter of hours disappear through nuclear annihilation or due to an extinction that plays out more slowly and just as inexorably as an overheated planet spins towards death.

The pieces assembled for this book were published in an array of American venues (*The New York Times, The Los Angeles Times*, CNN, *Time, The Nation, The Atlantic*, Tomdispatch, Salon, *The Modern Language Association Journal, The New Statesman*, the BBC, *Guernica*), as well as some foreign papers, especially in Brazil and Spanish speaking countries. Most appeared as commentaries on Trump's campaign, his election, and his occupation of the White House. Others, a select few, come from before the Trump era but have been included due to their ongoing relevance, though they have been revised and updated.

All of them try, in one way or another, to exorcise America, to see the specter of Donald Trump as a manifestation and ex-crescence of something deep in our country's desires and dreads and hatreds, and that will remain as a challenge no matter what happens, in the short run or long run. Trump came to power because he expressed what far too many of his countrymen wished for themselves and for their land. That America, Trump's America, will remain with us as a challenge whether Trump is impeached or survives to wreak more havoc, a challenge that I believe can only be met if the country undergoes a process of painful self-scrutiny that is impossible unless it is stimulated and accompanied by a new American revolution.

That is why, perhaps, these messages are also animated by another sort of ghost, the ghost of hope, incarnated and reimag-ined by multitudes of men and women and even children who have already shown that they will not surrender their right to battle for the future.

The thoughts I have gathered here are my small contribution to that battle. They were written, day by day, and during long nights of insomnia, against hopelessness and despair, with the burning conviction that understanding the world is imperative if we are to change it, if we are ever to reach the sweetness of a common dawn that Wordsworth envisioned for humanity.

May the fields of grief indeed be full of miracles.

PART ONE

THE RISE OF DONALD J. TRUMP

1.

PHILLIP II, THE SIXTEENTH CENTURY SPANISH MONARCH, WRITES TO HIS EXCELLENCY DONALD TRUMP

A MEDIUM THAT MY WIFE AND I CONSULT FREQUENTLY IN Chile intercepted a message from the 16th-century Spanish monarch Philip II directed to Donald Trump, words I transcribe here with, I must admit, some trepidation:

I, Philip II, the most powerful ruler of my time, have been watching, most excellent Señor Trump, the woes plaguing your nation, not dissimilar to those that I faced, as did my father, Carlos V, and my son, Philip III, in our own land. Economic decline, pandemics of poor people seeking free lunches, Christianity under siege from deviants and lax women, traditional values undermined by foreign-influenced intellectuals, distant enemies incessantly challenging you abroad while, at home, terrorist Muslims pretend to be peaceful citizens—troubles that we solved in our time with remedies that may prove beneficial to your own future reign.

Regarding the overseas potentates that threaten your hegemony, you should refrain from the temptation of negotiating with them. Like us, you have lethal weapons at your disposal and invincible armadas able to sail from bases on every continent. Take, therefore, the war to your enemy, decimate his cities, fields and, above all, his communications systems. Make him and his children tremble at the trumpet of your very name.

First though, deal with the enemies inside, who reproduce like rabbits. You have already proposed registering Muslims, something we did with severe efficiency, forcing them to wear badges and cease their infidel practices. If this measure turns out to be insufficient, you should deport them. Do not listen to those who declare that this will bring economic ruin and ignominy to the realm, nor that it cannot be physically accomplished. In a mere two years—from 1609 to 1611—my son managed (with the help of a heavily armed local militia) to be rid of this pestilent rabble, purifying Spain as you should purge America.

And while you're contemplating such a defense of national security, why not register the unruly poor as well, making sure they really deserve the charity so liberally lavished on them? I started with the beggars, decreeing in 1558 that only those veritably infirm could request alms, forcing the rest to work for their bread instead of rioting and chanting slogans. Though not all begging should be forbidden. When your students, like ours, accumulate calamitous financial obligations, they should be licensed to seek help in designated public areas. Besides such festive youngsters cheering up the populace with their antics, the budgetary cuts will liberate funds better destined to military expeditions.

And talking of education, why not introduce as an obligatory text in your schools, *The Perfect Housewife*, a manual, fashionable in our time, which counseled young women to obey their husbands, no matter how abusive, drunk, cruel, and irritable they might be. A discrete way to restore the natural hierarchy that God has created among species and sexes.

And if current domestic insubordination were to contaminate the republic itself, consider the possibility of resurrecting the Holy Brotherhood of the Inquisition. You have already suggested that you believe your enemies should be subjected to more extreme measures than mere waterboarding. How about fire? Nothing provides a fearful nation with more security than a select number of Auto da Fes, assisted by a surveillance system that already rivals mine, the envy of the nations of my time. And make sure the sword of justice is swift so that a death penalty constantly delayed by litigation is not rendered useless as a deterrent.

As to violent variations in the climate, do not heed demands that you intervene. Such scourges are God's way of testing your convictions. Instead of trying to cleanse the earth, cleanse your bodies and souls of sinfulness, in particular dealing with sodomites mercilessly. The Lord will respond with fresh air and sparkling water.

One last recommendation. During my reign, I considered the Jews to be Satanic, and was always grateful to my grandparents for expelling them from Spain in 1492. But I admit that there is one policy of their descendants in the Holy Land that I admire and suggest you imitate: build walls, many, many walls.

With best wishes, *mejores deseos*, to you and your future subjects, suggesting, just in case, that you share these thoughts with Mr. Cruz, whose very name evokes the Cross our Savior bore and which thrills our Christian soul,

Philip II, the Prudent King

2.

AMERICA MEETS FRANKENSTEIN

WHO CREATED DONALD TRUMP, WHO BREATHED SO MUCH life into him?

In order to explain the origins of the New York contender's astonishing run for the Presidency, many politicians and pundits have persistently recurred to Frankenstein, one of the founding myths of modernity, the story of a colossal monster who rises up and rebels against his maker. These observers point to the toxic political climate engendered by the Republicans over the last decades, Trump as the extreme incarnation of an incendiary stoking of fear, racism, and xenophobia, a misbegotten monster come home to roost.

The easy formula that equates Trump to the Monster and his Party to his Maker, irrefutable as it may be, does not, however, help us address the urgent problem of how to prevent the belligerent billionaire from prevailing.

For that, we need to turn to the novel *Frankenstein*, first conceived two hundred years ago in the dismal summer of 1816 by a young woman called Mary Shelley. And we should read it in a way that spurs us to go beyond the simplification to which her complex and cautionary tale of hubris has been reduced and confined by popular culture.

I admit to having succumbed, as a child of seven, to the pleasures of that simplification.

It was 1949 and I had just seen *Abbott and Costello Meet Frankenstein,* and I can remember gripping my mother's hand tight as we returned from the cinema in Manhattan to our house in Queens, not far from where Donald Trump, then three years old, was growing up in indubitably more opulent circumstances. I imagine that Trump might have reacted to the fiend by punching him in the face or carrying him out on a stretcher, but I confess that I was scared out of my wits. But I was also fascinated, determined to surmount my apprehension by visiting his every available avatar, from James Whale's film version to the sequels, *Bride of Frankenstein* and *Son of Frankenstein*, and even *The Ghost of Frankenstein*, where Lon Chaney took over from the perennial Boris Karloff.

My mother did not mind taking me to gorge myself on these shows as long as I promised, once I came of age, to read the original novel where I'd discover that Frankenstein, my Mom said, "is not the monster but rather the arrogant genius who designed him. And that will open up issues that have no facile answers." And, in effect, I did go to the source in late adolescence and was indeed tormented by a question that must have haunted Mary Shelley when, vacationing in a Swiss villa with Lord Byron and her future husband, Percy Bysshe Shelley, she began writing *Frankenstein*: who is the real monster, the unwilling creature who has been granted a deformed life or his overreaching creator?

Raising that anguishing question again today lets us delve deeper into what is truly terrifying in the Trump insurgency: the fact that immense legions are voting for a man who feeds on fear and relishes torture and mass deportation. Without these troubled multitudes who project onto him their uncertainties, nightmares, and desires, Trump would not exist. Aren't the real monsters, therefore, the men and women enthralled by his outrageous charisma, his strong arm bullying, his celebration of greed and manliness?

The temptation to build a wall around those people, to get them out of our sight and our lives, is often overwhelming. All the more reason to be wary of imitating his supporters, degrading and demonizing them as if they were invasive, malignant aliens.

It is precisely this dehumanization of the Other that Mary Shelley's novel critiques. Though most film versions portray the monster as speechless, in the book he has a delicate and despairing soul, and he is able to articulate his loneliness, demanding that he not be judged by his outer deformities. Am I being naïve to suggest that what we should feel for Trump's devotees is compassion? Leaving aside the violent, irredeemable fringes of fanatical bigots and neo-Nazis, can we not venture that the huge majority of Trump voters dwell in an existential desolation that is encapsulated in the epigraph from Milton's *Paradise Lost* that is quoted on the title page of *Frankenstein*, Adam's plea to the God that fashioned him: "Did I solicit thee/From darkness to promote me?"

His followers may have created Trump and fostered his rise, but which merciless God was it that promoted them from darkness and made these men and women feel so anxious about their families, so helpless and lost in their abandonment, that they would exalt a demagogue who appeals to their vilest instincts and thrives on their sorrow and insecurity?

Whether Trump is ultimately defeated or not, those masses of our misguided fellow citizens will remain vastly among us. They pose the real challenge. It was the darker side of America that spawned them, that facilitated their need for a Superman savior like Trump, so it must be the other, more luminous America, that should, after looking deep into the mirror, contest and defuse the wrath of so many frustrated millions, convincing them to stop conjuring up false demons from the abyss and start confronting the all too tangible demons of war, poverty, racism, inequality of gender, and ecological catastrophe that threaten us all, the true terrors and monsters we must vanquish side by side.

Only if we find a way of stripping the backers of Trump of their delusions and dread, only if we find a way to include them in the solution to the shared dilemmas of our time, will the last words of Mary Shelley's novel, as she bids farewell to the Monster and what is monstrous in us, deserve the slim chance of coming true, turning these lines into a wondrous prophecy: "He was soon borne away by the waves, and lost in darkness and distance."

3.

MY MOTHER AND TRUMP'S BORDER

DONALD TRUMP, REACTING TO A SPATE OF RECENT TERROR attacks, called on the government and law enforcement to fight, McCarthy-like, the "cancer from within." He then went on to exclaim: "How they came into the country in the first place is beyond me." Obviously, he believes that these and thousands of other possible (and according to him, inevitable) assailants did not undergo the "extreme vetting" that he proposed as indispensable to keep Muslim terrorists and those advocating Sharia law from entering the United States. Whether this prospective weeding out of aliens at the border, a process antagonistic to American values, would bolster our security is doubtful.

A long time ago my mother, Fanny Zelicovich Dorfman, who, alas, has not been alive for some 20 years, fell afoul of a system of interrogation similar to the one the Republican candidate wishes to put into place. Her story might provide a sober perspective on the pitfalls and traps that such examinations entail.

Though Fanny would later recount her detention by immigration officials lightheartedly, as was her wont when tragedies descended upon the family (and they were many), there was nothing amusing about the episode when it occurred.

My sister and I found out about my mother's mishap when, on the last day of our stay at Camp Tevya in Massachusetts—it must have been some time in late July or maybe August 1953—my parents did not turn up to retrieve us. Instead, my father asked some nearby friends in Boston to take care of us while he sorted out the mess his wife found herself in.

The problem started because my mother, having accompanied my dad on a trip to Europe that summer, decided not to fly back with him but instead to take a leisurely boat ride to the States, where our Argentine family had resided for the last nine years, most of them with a diplomatic visa, as my father was a high-ranking official of the United Nations. Which meant she was by herself when she confronted the immigration authorities.

They had begun by asking her the usual questions about her name (are you now or have you ever been known by any other legal names?), her address, and her resident status and then, perhaps emboldened by the McCarran Act that had been passed the previous year despite President Truman's veto, they went on to probe other aspects of her identity.

"Are you now or have you ever been a member of the Communist Party?"

It was simple for my mother to answer that. She rarely disagreed with my father about anything, but regarding communism she had demurred from his fervent Bolshevik sympathies, though she always did so gently, and with humor. At the dinner table she would announce, with a mischievous twinkle in her eye, that she had founded an organization called the SRCL-Communist Party—the Slightly Reformed Conservation Life Communist Party of which she was the chairman, secretary, treasurer, and sole member. So she answered, truthfully, that no, she was not currently nor had she ever been a member of the totalitarian group that the immigration functionaries were seeking to exclude from America.

"Do you advocate the overthrow of the government of the United States by force or subversion?"

The question was ridiculous, but my mother bit her tongue. She did not tell them that she loved many things about America (she adored Roosevelt), to the point of having contemplated becoming a citizen, but that the Red Scare, the House Un-American Activities Committee, Joseph McCarthy's quest for ideological purity, and the hounding of her own husband and many of his friends now made the country unpalatable, so much so that we were already planning to move to Chile. But what was the point of getting into an argument with these people?

"No," she said. "Of course not."

And then came the clincher:

"Do you intend to assassinate the president of the United States?"

My mother could not help herself. She laughed at the absurdity of the question. All she wanted to do was get off the boat and join my father and drive north to pick up her two kids. She thought a jest might lighten the proceedings.

"If I was going to assassinate the president, would I tell you?"

Confident that her charm—which was indeed prodigious—would get her through any thorny situation, she was surprised when they blocked her entry to the United States and sent her to Ellis Island for further investigation of her subversive and possible lethal activities. Her protests that she had been joking were met with a grim response: "This is no laughing matter, Mrs. Dorfman."

Family lore and her own storytelling aptitude—always ready to augment any incident, inflating it to epic proportions—has it that she spent three nights and days in detention, but my guess is that it was not more than 24 hours. What is true is that the Secretary General of the United Nations, Dag Hammarskjöld, had to intervene personally to convince the United States authorities that Fanny Zelicovich Dorfman was no threat to the security or future of the nation nor to the health and well-being of its president.

Sixty-three years later, as we endure another era dominated by fear of what is foreign and different—Muslims instead of Reds as the enemy, Sharia Law instead of doctrinaire Marxism as the target—my mother's encounter with those inquisitors and their queries offers anecdotal proof that the form of extreme vetting proposed by Donald Trump, besides being unconstitutional, would end up snaring innocent people like her at the border while letting seasoned criminals slip by undeterred. Those who are truly determined to destroy America will undoubtedly hide their objectives (or did they not undergo extensive training?), and those who are naïve enough to make a joke about our current paranoia will be delivered unto the inefficient hands of Homeland Security.

And that, in effect, is no laughing matter.

4.

LATIN AMERICAN FOOD
AND THE FAILURE OF TRUMP'S WALL

ONALD TRUMP HAS BUILT HIS CAMPAIGN AROUND THE threat posed to the United States by the "aliens" who have swarmed across the border from Mexico and who are, according to his tirades, a bunch of "bad hombres," rapists, criminals, and drug dealers. Though, of course, he has made a point of attesting to his love for Hispanics by tweeting a photo of himself eating a taco in Trump Tower Grill in order to celebrate Cinco de Mayo. Given his tenuous grasp of his own country's history, there can be no doubt that he does not know that Cinco de Mayo commemorates the defeat of a foreign enemy, France, back in 1862. A pity, because he would do well to ponder the traits with which the commander of the Mexican army characterized the head of the invading troops: arrogance, foolishness, and ineptitude—soberbia, necedad, y torpeza.

These are the very features Trump is exhibiting as he munches his taco and dreams of deporting (at least) eleven million "illegals" and building a huuuge and beautiful wall to keep them from ever coming back, and promises his rabid supporters that the colossal barrier with which he intends to divide the two countries will be paid for by Mexico.

What Trump does not seem to realize is that this is a battle he has already lost. No, I am not talking about the unfeasibility of constructing parts of his wall in the middle of the immense Rio Grande, shared by both countries. Or how he would need to defile sacred Native American land. Or the requirement that the wall be transparent enough to see the other side and simultaneously made of materials dense enough to withstand erosion and therefore opaque. Or what an impossible engineering feat it would be to rise high enough to keep out drones and deep enough to discourage tunnels that, so far, have thwarted every effort to be blocked. No, I am talking about a more modest foe of his proposal. Even before the first brick is laid, his wall was vanquished by the very taco he grins at demonically in his Twitter post, vanquished by that taco and its many food cousins from all over Latin America.

What? Food as the unsung hero, ready to foil Trump's dream of an ethnically pure America?

As proof of what some readers may consider a startling assertion, I offer a store that my wife and I frequent here in Durham, North Carolina, where we have settled after decades of wandering. I am sure that Trump's campaign will not bring him to this town where Barack Obama received 75.9% of the votes in 2012, the highest victory in the whole state. But if the Donald, a former wrestler who claims to relish a good brawl, were indeed to venture into this adversarial territory, I would recommend that he stop by this supermarket that Angélica and I visit, at times for convenience's sake but more often to indulge in personal nostalgia.

I can savor under its vast roof the presence of the continent where I was born, going back, so to speak, to my own plural origins. On one shelf, Nobleza Gaucha, the yerba mate my Argentine parents used to sip every morning in their New York exile—my mother with sugar, my father in its more bitter version. Even to contemplate the bag that this grass herb comes in, allows me to recall how anxiously mi mamá y mi papá awaited shipments from the authoritarian Buenos Aires they had escaped in the forties. A bit further along in the store, I come upon leche condensada en una lata, the sort I would sip from a can on adolescent camping trips into the mountains of Chile, where my family moved when I was twelve. And nearby, a tin of Nido, the powdered milk my wife Angélica and I first fed our son Rodrigo as a baby, almost half a century ago in Santiago. Or Nesquik para niños, the chocolate we relied on to sweeten the existence of our younger son Joaquín, when he accompanied us back to Chile after many years of banishment from Pinochet's dictatorship.

Origins, however, are never merely personal, but deeply collective, and especially so for Latin Americans such as myself, who feel an entrañable fellowship with natives from other unfortunate countries of our region. A stubborn history of thwarted dreams has led to a shared sense of purpose and sorrow, hope and resilience, which joins us all emotionally, beyond geographic destiny or national boundaries. To stroll up and down the grocery aisles of that store is to reconnect with the people and the lands and the tastebuds of those brothers and sisters and to partake, however vicariously, in meals being planned and prepared at that very moment in millions and millions of homes everywhere in the hemisphere. There is canela from Perú and queso crema from Costa Rica and café torrado e moido (O sabor do campo na sua casa) from Brasil. There is coconut juice from the Caribbean and frijoles of every possible and impossible variety and maíz tostado from Mexico and fresh apio/celery from the Dominican Republic (they look like tiny twisted idols) and hierbas medicinales para infusiones from who knows where, and albahaca and ajonjoli and linaza and yuca and malanga and chicharrones de cerdo and chicharrones de harina.

If you were to go to Sao Paulo or Caracas or Quito, if you were to try to shop for this assortment of staples or delicacies in San José or La Paz or Bogotá, if you were to ask in any major or minor city of Latin America where you might be able to pick your way through such a plethora of culinary choices in one location, you would be told that a place like that does not exist anywhere in that country. There is no shop in Rio de Janeiro, for instance, that next to an array of carioca fare would allow you to select among eighteen multiplicities of chile peppers or buy Tampico punch or sample some casabe bread.

That is what is most fascinating about this grocery store sporting the name COMPARE—a name which cleverly works in Spanish and English and Portuguese. Who would have thought that in a small town of the Southern United States (population 267,587) there could be a greater representation of variegated Latin America than in Rio with its six and a half million inhabitants or in the megapolis of Ciudad de México with its twenty million?

This is what Donald Trump and his nativist cohorts need to understand: five hundred and twenty-four years after Cristobal Colón sighted the land that would be called by some other visionary's name, the sheer reality of a store like this one (and countless others like it all across the United States), resoundingly proves that the continent of Juárez and García Márquez and Eva Perón can no longer be understood to stop at the Rio Grande but extends far into the gringo North.

The food that hails me at that mega-Latino supermarket is not, of course, purely something that you sniff and peel, cook and devour. Hands reach for the potatoes that originated thou sands of years ago in the Andean highlands, mouths water for the pineapple that the conquistadors did not know how to describe, bodies tremble at the thought of using their tongues, Proust-like, to return to a childhood home most of them will never see again. Behind hands and inside mouths and beyond bodies, there flourishes a cosmic piñata of stories, like mine, of escaping the native land, of alighting elsewhere, of crossing frontiers legally or surreptitiously, of border guards and guardian angels, of fighting to keep in touch with the vast pueblo latinoamericano left behind, of memories of hunger and repression, and also of solidaridad and vivid dreams. A woman from Honduras is piling onto her cart a ton of bananas that are the color of a red sunset and, though well on their way to decomposing, will be perfect, she assures me, with tomatillos and pinto frijoles. A couple from Colombia (I detect the soft specificity of excellent Spanish from Bogotá) discuss whether to experiment and add to their ajiaco that night some Mexican Serrano Peppers (shining green as they curve under the neon light). The husband says that's fine, so long as she doesn't forget to mix in the guascas herb they have just bought and which he first relished when he was an infant. Inside each of them, as inside me and my Angélica, there is a tale of heartbreak and heart warmth, of hearths orphaned back home and hearths rekindled in our new dwellings.

Where else could these shoppers (and so many other unrecognized ambassadors from every country and ethnicity of the Americas) meet in such an ordinary way, chatting in every conceivable Spanish accent (and some murmur to each other in indigenous tongues I cannot identify) next to this Chilean-American born in Argentina as if nothing could be more natural?

How many of them are threatened with concentration camps and deportations and families sundered, how many of these compatriots of ours are adrift and in danger of living on the borders of legality? I dare not ask. But what is certain, what I can proclaim from the haven of this pungent paradise full of undocumented food, is that the men and women who make this country work, who build the houses and pave the roads, who clean the houses and cook the meals and care for the children, who come from every one of our twenty-one Latin American republics and who only meet here in los Estados Unidos de América, what I can unequivocally declare is that they are not going away.

Your wall, Señor Trump, has already been breached, your wall has already been defeated by our peaceful invasion.

Along with our food, we are here to stay.

5.

—————

FAULKNER'S QUESTION FOR AMERICA

DOES AMERICA DESERVE TO SURVIVE?

That is the question that William Faulkner publicly posed in 1955 when news reached him that Emmett Till, a 14-year-old black youth, had been murdered and mutilated in a town in Mississippi for having dared to whistle at a married white woman—a lynching that acted as a catalyst for the creation of the civil rights movement.

Whether America deserves to survive was not the question I had expected to be asking myself on this literary pilgrimage that my wife and I had taken to Oxford, Mississippi, where Faulkner lived most of his life and wrote the torrential masterpieces that made him the most influential American novelist of the 20th century. We had been planning such a journey for many years, seeing it as a chance to meditate on the life and works of an author who had dared me since my Chilean adolescence to break all conventions, to venture every risk, in order to portray the multiple flow of time and mind and grief, who goaded me into trying to express what it means "to be alive and know it" in one of the remote backwaters of the wide world. And yet, it is that question about the survival of America that haunts me as we visit the grave at St. Peter's Cemetery where Faulkner was lowered into the earth 54 years ago, it crops up as we walk the streets he walked, it cannot be avoided as we wander through Rowan Oak, the antebellum mansion he called home.

Because if Faulkner were alive today, as his country faces "an incomprehensible moment of terror," the most drastic election of our maelstrom era, where an egomaniacal demagogue could conceivably occupy the White House, the author of *The Sound and the Fury* would surely once again painfully hurl that question about the future of the United States at his fellow citizens. And also, I have no doubt, he would issue a challenge to Trump's supporters, hoping that they, like so many of his own characters, will not doom themselves and their land to destruction out of rage and frustration, subjected to the darkness of an untamed past.

Faulkner's words today would not be addressed to African Americans, though he wrote of their dilemma with remarkable sensitivity, describing how the descendants of slaves carried, "with stern and inflexible pride," the burden imposed upon them by a corrosive and unjust system. But a man who preached patience as a way to overcome race barriers, a man who did not hear Martin Luther King's speeches, a man who could not have imagined even the possibility of a president born of miscegenation and even less of a Black Lives Matter movement (not to mention Oprah Winfrey!), would have little to teach a multicultural America that he would find unrecognizable. Equally difficult for him to deal with would be the women empowered by the feminist revolutions he could not have anticipated.

Other, less enviable, aspects of contemporary America would, however, be more sadly familiar to Faulkner.

He would have been appalled, but not in the least surprised, by the rise of Donald Trump or the deranged danger he represents. Faulkner had created in his fictional universe a minor Southern incarnation of Trump: Flem Snopes, an unscrupulous and voracious predator with "eyes the color of stagnant water" who claws and lies his wily way to power, cheating and conning anyone naïve enough to think they can outsmart him. In Flem and his clan, Faulkner excoriated many of his fellow citizens who "know and believe in nothing but money and it doesn't much matter how you get it." He harbored no doubt about the harm people like the Snopes tribe could inflict if allowed to reign and proliferate, if their "stupid chicanery and petty corruption for stupid and petty ends" were ever to prevail. Given the latest polls, such an electoral apocalypse seems increasingly unlikely, but the mere fact that Trump is even a viable candidate, would be terrifying to the author of *Absalom, Absalom*!

Faulkner would have understood why so many of his fellow citizens feel that they are trapped in a historical tide not of their making, that their American dream has gone berserk.

Though politically liberal and progressive for his time, Faulkner's attitude toward the Donald's followers would have been, therefore, sympathetic. He lovingly and often good-humoredly portrayed the lives of those whom we might identify today, forgiving the generalization, as core Trump supporters—hunters and gun owners; ill-informed men clinging to their threatened virility and old time traditions; white Americans of small rural or economically depressed communities overwhelmed by the harsh rush of modernity, unprepared for a globalization they cannot control. Without ever condoning their racial prejudices and paranoia he also never condescended to them, never looked down upon their bafflement and blindness, always afforded them the one thing they deeply desired then and still desire now: respect for their human dignity. Faulkner would have understood the roots of the present disaffection of those people he cared for so much and the fear from which that disaffection is derived.

This is what makes Faulkner so valuable a voice today.

The empathy that this extraordinary, sophisticated novelist felt for the less educated, religiously conservative inhabitants of his imaginary county of Yoknapatawpha and their sense of loss and disorientation, the fact that he preferred their enduring and dignified company to the abstractions and elitism of privileged intellectuals, makes him ideally suited for delivering a message that Trump's devotees should try to heed, a plea against bigotry and dread and divisiveness that is not tainted with even a hint of paternalism or contempt.

As I contemplate the fragile, tiny desk in his study at Rowan Oak where he composed the words for his daughter Jill's high school graduation, I can hear the echo of these words today, and am honored to convey them once more to Faulkner's present day compatriots. He urged his daughter's class, and urges us right now, to become like "men and women, who will refuse always to be tricked or frightened or bribed into surrendering." He told them, and tells us again and yet again, that we have not just the right, "but the duty too, to choose between...courage and cowardice..." He speaks to me and to them and to all of us when he demands to "never be afraid to raise your voice for honesty and truth and compassion, against injustice and lying and greed."

Will we stumble and falter into the abyss, come to grief?

Are we doomed to tragedy, like so many of Faulkner's relentless characters, or do we still have the chance and wisdom to prove that this country deserves to survive?

PART TWO

THE JUDGMENT OF HISTORY

6.

NOW, AMERICA,
YOU KNOW HOW CHILE FELT

T IS FAMILIAR, THE OUTRAGE AND ALARM THAT MANY
Americans ARE feeling at reports that Russia, according to a
secret intelligence assessment, interfered in the United States
election to help Donald J. Trump become president

I have been through this before, overwhelmed by a similar
outrage and alarm.

To be specific: on the morning of Oct. 22, 1970, in what was
then my home in Santiago de Chile, my wife Angélica and I
listened to a news flash on the radio. General René Schneider,
the head of Chile's armed forces, had been shot by a commando
on a street of the capital. He was not expected to survive.

Angélica and I had the same automatic reaction: it's the CIA,
we said, almost in unison. We had no proof at the time—though
evidence that we were right would eventually, and abundantly,
surface—but we did not doubt that this was one more American
attempt to subvert the will of the Chilean people.

Six weeks earlier, Salvador Allende, a democratic Socialist, had won the presidency in a free and fair election, in spite of the United States' spending millions of dollars on psychological warfare and misinformation to prevent his victory (we'd call it "fake news" today). Allende had campaigned on a program of social and economic justice, and we knew that the government of President Richard M. Nixon, allied with Chile's oligarchs, would do everything it could to stop Allende's nonviolent revolution from gaining power.

The country was rife with rumors of a possible coup. It had happened in Guatemala and Iran, in Indonesia and Brazil, where leaders opposed to United States interests had been ousted. Now it was Chile's turn. That was why General Schneider was assassinated. Because, having sworn loyalty to the Constitution, he stubbornly stood in the way of those destabilization plans.

General Schneider's death did not block Allende's inauguration, but American intelligence services, at the behest of Henry A. Kissinger, continued to assail our sovereignty during the next three years, sabotaging our prosperity ("make the economy scream," Nixon ordered) and fostering military unrest. Finally, on Sept. 11, 1973, Allende was overthrown and replaced by a vicious dictatorship that lasted nearly 17 years. Years of torture and executions and disappearances and exile.

Given all that pain, one might presume that some glee on my part would be justified at the sight of Americans squirming in indignation at the spectacle of their democracy subjected to foreign interference—as Chile's democracy, among many other countries, was by America. And yes, it is ironic that the CIA—the very agency that gave not a whit for the independence of other nations—is now crying foul because its tactics have been imitated by a powerful international rival.

I can savor the irony, but I feel no glee. This is not only because, as an American citizen myself now, I am once again a victim of this sort of nefarious meddling. My dismay goes deeper than that personal sense of vulnerability. This is a collective disaster: those who vote in the United States should not have to suffer what those of us who voted in Chile had to go through. Nothing warrants that citizens anywhere should have their destiny manipulated by forces outside the land they inhabit.

The seriousness of this violation of the people's will must not be flippantly underestimated or disparaged.

When Mr. Trump denies, as do his acolytes, the claims by the intelligence community that the election was, in fact, rigged in his favor by a foreign power, he is bizarrely echoing the very responses that so many Chileans got in the early '70s when we accused the CIA of illegal interventions in our internal affairs. He is using now the same terms of scorn we heard back then: those allegations he says, are "ridiculous" and mere "conspiracy theory," because it is "impossible to know" who was behind it.

In Chile, we did find out who was "behind it." Thanks to the Church Committee and its valiant, bipartisan 1976 report, the world discovered the many crimes the CIA had been committing, the multiple ways in which it had destroyed democracy elsewhere—in order, supposedly, to save the world from Communism.

This country deserves, as all countries do—including Russia, of course—the possibility of choosing its leaders without someone in a remote room abroad determining the outcome of that election. This principle of peaceful coexistence and respect is the bedrock of freedom and self-determination, a principle that, yet again, has been compromised—this time, with the United States as its victim.

What to do, then, to restore faith in the democratic process?

First, there should be an independent, transparent, and thorough public investigation so that any collusion between American citizens and foreigners bent on mischief can be exposed and punished, no matter how powerful these operatives may be. The president-elect should be demanding such an inquiry, rather than mocking its grounds. The legitimacy of his rule, already damaged by his significant loss of the popular vote, depends on it.

But there is another mission, a loftier one, that the American people, not politicians or intelligence agents, must carry out. The implications of this deplorable affair should lead to an incessant and unforgiving meditation on our shared country, its values, its beliefs, its history.

The United States cannot in good faith decry what has been done to its decent citizens until it is ready to face what it did so often to the equally decent citizens of other nations. And it must firmly resolve never to engage in such imperious activities again.

If ever there was a time for America to look at itself in the mirror, if ever there was a time of reckoning and accountability, it is now.

7.

THE RIVER KWAI PASSES THROUGH LATIN AMERICA AND THE POTOMAC: WHAT IT FEELS LIKE TO BE TORTURED

WHEN DONALD TRUMP PROMISED THAT, IF ELECTED President, he would "bring back a hell of a lot worse than waterboarding," I could not help but remember a man I met twenty-two years ago, not in my native Latin America or in faraway lands where torture is endemic, but in the extremely English town of Berwick-upon-Tweed.

Everybody in the room that day was crying, everybody except for the man who had moved us all to tears, the former prisoner of war whom my son Rodrigo and I had traveled thousands of miles to meet. We had hoped to do justice to his story in a biopic, *Prisoners in Time*, that the BBC wanted to make for television, based on his autobiography, *The Railway Man*.[1]

---

1 Many years after we wrote the BBC film, which received the 1995 Writers Guild of Great Britain Award for Best Television Screenplay, *The Railway Man*, a movie starring Colin Firth and Nicole Kidman based on the same autobiographical material, was shown on many screens. There is no relationship between that movie and our television biopic.

And what an extraordinary story it was!

Eric Lomax, a British officer in World War II, had been tortured by the Japanese in Thailand while working on the infamous Bangkok-Burma railroad, the one most people know about through another film, *The Bridge on the River Kwai*. Eric, like so many victims of atrocities, was plagued by the experience, his life destroyed by memories of his agony and the desire for revenge. What differentiated him from so many others persecuted worldwide was not only that, more than forty years later, he tracked down the man he held responsible for his suffering, the anonymous interpreter at his beatings and waterboardings, but the astounding fact that this tormentor, Takashi Nagase, once he was found and identified, turned out to be a Buddhist monk. Nagase had spent the postwar decades denouncing his own countrymen for their crimes and trying to atone for his role in the atrocities he had helped commit by caring for innumerable orphans of the Asians who had died building the railroad. The one scorching image from the war he could not escape was that of a brave young British lieutenant over whose torture he had presided and whom he had presumed to be dead.

Once Eric Lomax resurfaced; once the two former enemies, now old men accompanied by their second wives, met in Kanchanaburi, next to the River Kwai, where they had last parted; once they were face to face, Nagase begged for forgiveness. It was not instantly forthcoming. But some weeks later, in Hiroshima of all places, Lomax offered Nagase the absolution that he needed in order to live and die in peace.

The BBC had chosen me to tell this tale because, in my play *Death and the Maiden,* I had already probed the issues of torture, memory, mercy, and vengeance from the perspective of our beleaguered country, Chile. But in that play there had been no pardon offered and no pardon sought, so writing about Lomax's dilemma seemed a way of furthering that original exploration with a series of new questions. Is reconciliation ever really possible when the wounds are searing and permanent? Does anything change if the victimizer claims to have repented? How can we ever know if those claims are legitimate, or if that remorse is merely an ego-trip, an accommodation for the sake of outward appearances?

There was also an aesthetic challenge: given the extreme reserve of both antagonists, their inability to articulate to one another—not to mention anybody else—what they had been feeling all these years, how was one to imagine for the screen the dialogue that our two silent former enemies never said but that would remain true to their affliction? How to bring that story to those who can't possibly imagine what torture does to those who suffer it and those who create that suffering?

Our visit to Eric and his wife Patti at their home in the far north of England was a way of trying to coax from that emotionally repressed man some information—entirely absent from the memoir he had written—about how he had dealt with the barren wilderness of his sorrow, what it meant to survive torture and war more dead than alive. We were accompanied by director Stephen Walker and celebrated psychiatrist Helen Bamberg, who had helped Eric name his demons, and so saved him and his troubled marriage.

That day, in Berwick-upon-Tweed, Eric confided to us, after several hours of halting monosyllables, a painful, unbelievable story. When he returned to England by ship after those traumatic years as a prisoner of war, he discovered just before disembarking that the British Army had deducted from his back pay the cost of the boots he had lost during his captivity. Bamberg, who had managed to get Eric to speak out after many distressing past sessions in London, asked him if he had told anyone about this at the time.

"Nobody," Eric said. And then, after a pause that felt infinite, "There was nobody there, at the dock." He stopped and again long minutes of silence went by before he added, "Only a letter from my father. Saying he had remarried, as my mother had died three years before." Another long pause followed. "She died thinking I was also dead. I had been writing to her all that time and she was dead."

That's when we all started to cry.

Not just out of sympathy for his grief, but also because Eric had delivered this story about his loss in a monotone devoid of any apparent sentiment, as if all that despair belonged to someone else. Such dissociation is typical of torture victims. Their mental survival during their ordeal and its unending aftermath depends on distancing themselves from their body and its fate. And it is in that distance that they dwell.

We were crying, I believe, for humanity. We were crying in the Lomax living room because we were being confronted with a reality and a realization that most people would rather avoid: when grievous harm has been done to someone, the damage may be beyond repair. Eric Lomax had been able to tame the hatred raging in his heart and, reaching into the deepest wells of compassion, he had forgiven one of the men who had destroyed him. And yet, there was still something irreparable, a terror that ultimately could not be assuaged.

The film we wrote back in 1994 tried to be faithful to that desolate moment of revelation and at the same time not betray the inner peace that Eric had attained, the fact that he no longer heard Nagase's voice in his nightmares demanding, "Confess, Lomax, confess and pain will stop." He had triumphed over fear and fury, but that spiritual victory had not been achieved in solitude. Besides his wife Patti's support, it was due to the healing process he had gone through with Helen Bamberg. Not until he had fully come to terms with what had been done to him, until he faced his trauma in all its horror, was he able to "find" Nagase, whose identity and location had, in fact, been within easy reach for decades.

Eric's tragedy and his attempt at reconciliation had a special meaning for me: it connected his life to that of so many friends in Chile and other countries who had been subjected to inhuman interrogations. It was a way of understanding the common humanity of all torture victims, especially since the method that Bamberg employed to resurrect Eric's memories and restore his mental health had first been elaborated as a therapeutic response to the flood of damaged Latin Americans exiled in England during the 1970s and 1980s when grim dictatorships dominated that continent. Eric Lomax, she said, had the sad privilege of being the first World War II veteran with PTSD who was able to take advantage of this new psychological treatment.

We could not know, of course, that 9/11 awaited us seven years in the future, that the waterboarding inflicted on Eric in the 1940s by the Japanese, and on the bodies of so many Latin Americans decades later by their own countrymen, would go global as the United States and its allies fought the "war on terror." Nor could we have guessed that so many millions in that future would prove so indifferent to a form of punishment that has been classified as a crime against humanity and is against international treaty and law signed onto by most of the world's nations.

It would seem, then, that Eric Lomax's story is today more relevant than ever—a story that, one would hope, brings home again the ultimate reality and anguish of being tortured. Or can we accept that the questions Eric Lomax asked himself about forgiveness and revenge, about redemption and memory, no longer trouble contemporary humanity?

How would our friend Eric, who died in 2012, react to the news that so many Americans and so many of the very countrymen he served in the war now declare torture to be tolerable, as recent polls indicate? What would he say to former Vice-President and war criminal Dick Cheney, who has reiterated over and over that "enhanced interrogations" have been and still are absolutely necessary to keep Americans safe? How would he answer the bluster of Donald Trump?

Perhaps he would whisper to all those who believe this horror is justified the words he wrote to Nagase when he forgave his enemy: "Sometime the hatred has to stop."

8.

WORDS OF ENCOURAGEMENT FOR DONALD J. TRUMP FROM JAMES BUCHANAN, 15TH PRESIDENT OF THE UNITED STATES

Sir:

How long have I waited for your advent, prayed for someone like you to come along? All these years, since my death in 1868, I have watched each election cycle, hoping that finally my savior would appear, a man—heaven forbid it should be a woman!—who would rescue me from my status as the worst president in the annals of the United States.

Limited as your knowledge of our past may be, surely you are aware that I have been blamed for the secession of the Southern states in 1861, just as my term was ending. Unfairly faulted for the Civil War that ensued, I am now relieved to know that the presidency will soon be in the hands of someone who will, I am certain, go down in history as a leader who most bitterly divided the nation and undermined the foundations of our democracy.

I am excited, indeed, about your chances of outshining me. If you persist in your campaign to drill, extract, and pollute, if you enable the climate deniers and help to overheat our spacious skies, you will have led us, not to the brink of a conflagration that killed a mere million, but to a more substantial achievement of worldwide significance: taking the whole of humanity to the brink of extinction. That is a record that will considerably exceed my own lapses and make me seem a paragon of wisdom to future citizens (at least, those who survive).

As to the peoples' daily lives, you are likely to far surpass the harm I have wrought there as well. Many families cursed my name as they received news of their maimed or dead kin, but many more will curse yours when their well-being deteriorates as you assault the country's healthcare system.

Regarding corruption, I am also hopeful you will outstrip me. My offenses (accused of bribery, extortion, and abuse of power by a congressional committee) will be deemed petty compared to those that loom for you, guaranteeing an administration rife, at all levels, with sleaze and conflicts of interest. But do not tarry over your manifest financial or ethical dilemmas. I managed to avoid impeachment and so will you, given your proven ability to convince your supporters that facts do not matter. Would that such talents had been bestowed upon me, and oh that television and social media had been invented in my day. I could have blamed Mexico for our Civil War.

Could you address two other matters? The first is abortion. It was during my presidency, in 1859, that the American Medical

Association urged the criminalization of women who terminated their pregnancies, and you have the chance to revert our laws and customs to that pristine moment when the gentle sex recognized that their bodies belonged to their menfolk. And then Cuba. I tried in vain to buy that island from Spain and then favored invading it. You can complete my dream. Extend the reach of our empire into the Caribbean and beyond, intervene vigorously in the affairs of enemy and allied nations. Pay special attention to China, where I made the mistake of being only marginally involved in the Second Opium War. I am sure you will do better when you engage the Chinese in the First Asian Trade War.

I am not alone in urging you to stubbornly follow your instincts. Other deceased presidents also entertain high expectations for your reign. Richard Nixon wishes that your slurs and insults would make people forget his own foul language, and he eagerly anticipates manifold Trumpgates that will make Watergate seem small potatoes. Warren G. Harding is certain that your outrages will go far beyond the Teapot Dome scandal, which fraudulently favored the oil companies. And Herbert Hoover, reviled for ignoring the oncoming Great Depression, is confident you will be even more obtuse, and that when you precipitate a worse economic catastrophe his actions will thus appear less disastrous. He expects you will also best him in union-busting and the massive deportation of immigrants.

Presidents who occupy the top tier of favorite leaders, including several Founding Fathers, have reproached me for appealing to what they call the worst angels of your nature. They are preparing a collective message counseling moderation and praying that you are not further deranged by the power of your high office.

Franklin Roosevelt believes that informing you that he regrets the internment of Americans of Japanese origin will discourage you from a roundup of Muslim Americans. Harry Truman, haunted by the ghosts of Hiroshima, would press you to abolish nuclear weapons instead of starting a devastating arms race. Dwight Eisenhower intends to reiterate his warning against the military-industrial complex—so naïve, our Ike, unable to realize that representatives of those powers are about to be blatantly ensconced in your Cabinet. And Mr. Lincoln, whose party you have terribly transmogrified, trusts that if he were to whisper daily guidance in your ear, the Republic might, once more, be saved.

I have no doubt that you will not heed him or any other meddling altruist.

After all, I send these words of encouragement inspired by your own example. You have taught me that it is better to bolster one's image in the Presidential Celebrity Sweepstakes than to sacrifice oneself for the good of the country.

And so, farewell, until the moment you join the former presidents on the other side of death, when I will be delighted to steer you to the very bottom of the heap, where I have languished for a century and a half. What a pleasure finally to be able to look down upon someone who has done damage to the United States in ways unimaginable to me in my most desolate dreams.

With my sincere thanks for all your efforts to rescue me from the nethermost abyss and from the title "worst of the worst," I remain, sir, your humble servant,

JAMES BUCHANAN

9.

A MESSAGE FROM THE END OF THE WORLD

ERE IN CHILE, IN THE FAR SOUTH OF THE SOUTHERN Hemisphere, it has been the summer of our discontent. Never have so many natural catastrophes in a row hit this country at the end of the world. For once, it is not the earthquakes that have assailed us since time immemorial or the tsunamis that often follow, devastating land and coast, mountainscapes and ocean. This time, our unprecedented woes have all been man-made.

First were the forest wildfires, mostly to the south of Santiago, the worst in recorded history. Countless acres have been burned to cinders, killing people and livestock, leveling a whole town, destroying centenarian trees as well as newer woodlands meant for export. The conflagration was not controlled until supertanker planes that could carry tons of water were flown in from abroad.

For those not directly threatened by the raging blazes, there were other costs. The air here in Santiago, befouled with smoke and ash, became unbreathable for weeks, a situation aggravated by inordinately high temperatures that did not diminish even at night, as was habitually the case, when we used to have the chance to cool off and face the next day refreshed and energized.

We prayed for rain, though we are aware that it never rains during the summer months. When our prayers were answered, it was not what we had expected. A deluge descended, not in the zones where the fires continued to flare up now and then, but deep in the Andes and its glaciers, and with such ferocity that rivers overflowed and avalanches of mud and debris descended on villages and valleys, roads and bridges.

As such a downpour had never come to pass before in the summer, the water-processing plants were distressingly unprepared. This left millions of Chileans without water in our homes, unable to drink, cook, clean, or bathe. It is as if we had been cursed with a plague: stray dogs expiring of thirst on the streets and plants withering and lines of people with buckets, wash basins, and bottles, standing endlessly in front of emergency distribution centers.

First so much fire that we cannot breathe, then so much water that we cannot drink. What comes next?

The news that many beaches in Chile have been closed as, once again after last year's plague, armadas of jellyfish wash up on the shores and fish perish. And then, there are the recent reports that a gigantic crack has deepened in an Antarctic ice shelf, increasing the possibility that an iceberg extending nearly

2,000 square miles will crash into the sea and, as it melts, alter forever the seascape of the planet, with Chile (whose territorial claim in that continent is governed by a treaty with six other nations) one of the first victims.

It is hardly strange, therefore, that Chile does not close its eyes to what is happening to our water, forests, and coastline. Everyone here—and I mean everyone, from extreme right to extreme left—understands that in this land, whose name comes from the Aymara language for the place where the earth ends, we are witnessing a cataclysm of epic proportions that presages another sort of end, the end of the world as we know it. And so we all are conscious that something just as epic must be done to change course before it is too late.

We also understand, of course, that such a change depends on what other international actors do elsewhere.

What is truly intolerable, what enrages and saddens me—as the fires rage in the forests and the rain falls when and where it should not and the rivers are choked with mudslides and the fish disappear from the ocean and the Antarctic breaks up—is what is transpiring simultaneously in the remote United States. Precisely at this dire moment in Chile's natural history, precisely now I am forced to watch how the government of the powerful country that my wife and I have adopted as our home is gutting the very environmental policies that, even if insufficient, were at least steps in the right direction.

As we get ready to return to the United States, our friends and relatives ask, over and over, can it be true? Can President

Trump be beset with such suicidal stupidity as to deny climate change and install an enemy of the earth as his environmental czar? Can he be so beholden to the blind greed of the mineral extraction industry, so ignorant of science, so monumentally arrogant, not to realize that he is inviting apocalypse? Can it be, they ask?

The answer, alas, is yes.

10.

SHOULD IAGO BE TORTURED?

OF ALL THE FICTIONAL CHARACTERS IN THE LITERARY universe, the malicious Iago, who betrays his commander and friend, Othello, leading to the doom of sweet Desdemona, may be the villain who most deserves the liquid fires of limitless punishment. Shakespeare's play leaves no doubt as to what awaits that "demi-devil": torture unto death. And the command is to make it slow: "If there be any cunning cruelty / that can torment him much and hold him long, / it shall be his."

The spectators watching *The Moor of Venice* when it was first performed in1604 were more than aware of what those torments entailed, having regularly attended executions conceived as public displays of brutality.

Just one notorious case, out of many, that would have been etched in the memory and eyes of London theatre-goers, was the martyrdom of Robert Southwell, a Jesuit priest and superb poet, whose verses ("My mind to me an empire is") were well known to Shakespeare. In February of 1595, Southwell, accused of treason, was strung up at Tyburn. Sentenced to be disemboweled while still alive, his corpse ended up quartered and his head cut off, exhibited to a large, ogling crowd. Before dying, Southwell wrote about his experience during three previous years of incarceration and dismay. Some of the prisoners, he says, "are hanged by the handes eight or nine houres, yea twelve houres together, till not only their wits, but even their senses fayle them." Additional horrors he describes are genital disfigurement and sleep deprivation; racks that roll the body into a ball and crush different parts until blood spurts out; and inmates so starved in dark dungeons that they lick "the very moisture off the walls".

What sets Othello's nemesis apart from Southwell and countless suspects in England and across Europe who were pressed to death with slabs, burned during interrogations and at the stake, and subjected to waterboarding was that Iago did not claim to be innocent, took pride in his perfidy. Nor did he have any willing accomplices in his conspiracy, so no actionable "intelligence" could be rooted out of his throat.

Why, then, afflict him in such a savage manner?

In our own presumably civilized century, where torture is held to be illegal, a crime against humanity, and yet practiced systematically all over the globe, including, until just a few years ago, by the United States in black sites abroad, the reasons for someone like Iago to be savagely tormented has enormous relevance and implications.

For starters, Iago's body must be mercilessly mutilated because the audience would have demanded that kind of retribution, cheering at the thought of that traitor on the rack, a minor redress of justice in a tragedy where few other comforts are on offer.

Another reason was to make an example of him and anyone else who might dare to attack the foundations of the State and the order of the universe. Indeed, the spectacular nature of that performance of pain was supposed, according to Queen Elizabeth the First herself, to be "for the terror of others."

The final reason is one Shakespeare may have found the most intriguing.

In Cinthio's novella, the source from which he had lifted the outlines of the story, multiple motives animate this dreadful Machiavellian schemer. Shakespeare went out of his way to jettison most of them. Shakespeare's Iago has not been demoted by Othello. Nor does he deem that Othello has seduced his wife or tarnished his reputation. Iago is an enigma, refusing to explain the whys and wherefores of his hatred, declaring in the last scene of the play that nobody will drag any clarity from him: "Demand me nothing. What you know you know. / From this time forth I will never speak word." And despite the ominous threat of one of his captors ("Torments will ope your lips"), we will not hear one more syllable from this "hellish villain."

Shakespeare tempts his audience, then and now, makes them yearn to crack open Iago's soul, watch it be cracked open so he can pour forth his secrets. Shakespeare shared, I submit, the sick curiosity humans have when confronted by the boundaries of something infinitely perverse. If we could only fathom the psyche that commanded such malignancy, we whisper to ourselves, then perhaps—it is a delusion, yet we persist in demanding and desiring it—we might recognize the next avatar of evil, stop him before he again sows chaos and wickedness in his wake.

Of course, most torture, back in Shakespeare's time and in ours, is perpetrated for less metaphysical purposes: primarily, as a way of wresting information from the suspect, to get him to confess his guilt, betray his network, reveal and prevent future atrocities.

Despite the Universal Declaration of Human Right having been adopted in 1948 (its article five stipulates that "No one shall be subjected to torture or to cruel, inhuman or degrading treatment or punishment"), despite ensuing treaties and conventions that outlaw such tribulations, despite the UN General Assembly unanimously proclaiming two decades ago that June 26th should be known as the International Day in Support of Victims of Torture, these violations of body and mind continue to be exculpated and justified by the idea that they save lives.

It does not seem to matter that there is incontrovertible evidence that torture does not work. Donald Trump vowed, during his campaign, to bring back waterboarding "and a hell of a lot worse," a position he suggested he might reconsider when James N. Mattis, soon to be his Defense Secretary, explained that such methods are useless and counterproductive. Still, all it would take is a major terrorist assault to revive such maltreatment. A recent survey indicated that almost half of Americans approved of the use of torture if it led to information being extracted.

I do not want to look down upon those multitudes of misguided, apprehensive fellow citizens. I understand the collective panic from which that blindness to the pain of the enemy stems, I commiserate with their thirst for a total, and sadly unobtainable, security.

Before we judge those millions of people, let us pause to reflect on our own reactions, our own imperfect humanity. When I am entangled in the emotions of *Othello*, distraught at innocence smothered and nobility murdered, I also wish to see Iago suffer without surcease for his sins. I suspect every other member of the contemporary audience feels, as I do, as the spectators in Shakespeare's theatre did, an indecent sense of satisfaction at imagining someone so serially and deviously evil being tormented without remission.

It is at moments like these, when we are trapped by the desire for reckoning and revenge, that we must remember the terrifying truth about Iago: he is human, all too human and enjoys, by the mere circumstance of having been born, certain inalienable rights. This monster who planned the ruin of Othello and the wondrous Desdemona with the deliberate cold passion of a suicide-bomber—with the same detached rationality and indifference of a general who drops mega-bombs on faraway women and children—happens, alas, to be a member of our species, an extreme litmus test for that species.

Only when we have the moral courage to declare that someone like Iago, especially someone foul like Iago, should not be put on the rack or have his genitals slashed or forced to open his lips and scream and scream, only then, only when we understand that hurting his howling and malignant body in this way degrades us all, will we have really advanced towards abolishing the plague of cunning cruelty from the earth.

I fear that day will be a long time coming.

11.

MISSION AKKOMPLISHED:
FROM COMRADE BUSH TO TOVARISCH TRUMP

A DECADE AGO, WHEN GEORGE W. BUSH WAS THE PRESI-
dential enigma that needed to be unraveled (yes, remember
when we used to ask ourselves how could somebody so bungling
and clueless and belligerent have been elected to the most powerful office in the world? Oh those were the days!), I found myself one morning trolling the Internet, looking for reasons why
the United States does not celebrate its workers the same day as
the rest of the world, even if the origins of that date happen to
be profoundly American: May 1st, 1886, when demands for an
eight hour workday by Chicago trade unions (mostly made up
of European immigrants) were met by violent police
repression.

When my search engine turned up an unknown website,
www.secrethistorygeorgewbush.com, I almost decided not to
explore its contents. Of all Americans, after all, the one least
likely to be linked to Mayday was the younger President Bush,

notoriously uninterested in history or, for that matter, the working class. The website, however, managed to make a connection, albeit an astounding one:

It has now been confirmed. May 1st 1973: that was the date George W. Bush was recruited as an agent by the KGB rather than sometime in 1972 as had been previously reported on this website. "As this is the son of George Herbert Walker Bush, the Chairman of the governing Republican party," the security officer in charge of the operation wrote to Secretary General Yuri Andropov in a coded message which has now been deciphered, "we will see where this leads. Take it as a gift to the glorious Soviet people on this International Workers' Day." Another source inside the Kremlin indicates that, upon receiving the news, the usually solemn Andropov smiled as he reviewed the troops marching through Red Square and murmured to his fellow members of the Politburo: "We have a secret weapon and it is not here in Moscow."

I blinked at the screen that day in 2006—or maybe it was 2007?

The next paragraph was even more absurd:

Jump forward thirty years, to May 1st 2003. There was George W. Bush, now the President, landing on the deck of the air craft carrier Abraham Lincoln and proclaiming, under a gigantic MISSION ACCOMPLISHED banner, that 'major combat operations' in Iraq had ceased. At first glance the event appeared as a fantastic Top Gun photo op on a vessel named after the greatest Republican President of all time, and that had just returned from the Second Gulf War without suffering a single casualty. The ship's home-coming had been delayed, idling thirty miles off the coast of California until the soft morning light was ready for the Commander in-Chief to fly in on an S-3B Viking jet, strut around in full battle gear and send a message to a world celebrating workers: the U.S. does not need you or your countries to rule this planet.

Or that was what Bush's American handlers thought was transpiring. This website, www.secrethistorygeorgewbush.com, can now confirm that the real message was intended for W's Russian handler, that the MISSION ACCOMPLISHED banner was a mischievous wink and nod to the President's very own KGB agent in charge of his activities: I did it, tovarisch. We're on our way. Watch what is about to happen in Iraq and elsewhere and enjoy the decline of the American empire. My jubilation knows no bounds. Happy Thirtieth Anniversary! Long live International Workers' Day!"

And suddenly, before I could click over to another website which might provide less ludicrous material about May 1st and America, my computer shut down, the words and very website vanishing from my eyes. Irritated by this freak mishap, I re-booted my Toshiba, brought Google up, and typed in the Internet address.

Unable to open http://www.secrethistorygeorgewbush. com/. Cannot locate Internet Server or proxy server.

I tried again.

Same outcome.

The following hour of clumsy surfing yielded no trace of that incongruous blog or anything approximating it. I asked my eldest son, Rodrigo, a webmaster himself, if he could find out whether *secrethistorygeorgewbush.com* was owned by anyone. A few minutes later he informed me that nobody had bought it or, as far as he could tell, ever used it. Did I want to secure that domain? And what was I up to anyway?

Not a bad question.

What was I up to?

I told my son that there was nothing amiss, I was just curious, forget the whole thing. But I could not, in fact, forget it at all. Was somebody playing a trick on me? Had I been hallucinating? Or had that abruptly cancelled website even existed? Brought up on Hitchcock's *The Lady Vanishes* as a child, spy novels as an adolescent, and the victim of real conspiracies as an adult, I could easily conjure up the anonymous author of such wild accusations seated in some smoke-filled interrogation room, even as the web police (whoever they might be) erased all remnants of those outlandish theories from the vast plateaus of virtual reality.

Stop right there. I needed to resist the temptations of political science fiction. What mattered about May 1st in 2006 (or was it 2007 or 2008?), in the United States, was that 120 or so years after those European immigrants had marched through the streets of Chicago, Mayday was being miraculously resurrected by other workers, by other immigrants. Hundreds of thousands of men and women would again fill those Chicago streets and streets all across America. But this time the workers would come primarily from Latin America, most of them illegal and all of them united against the impending legislation threatening to expel them. And they had chosen this date, an American date forgotten by America, to emerge from invisibility.

That was the story that mattered. The workers from the South bringing Mayday, the day known in Mexico as El Dia de los Mártires de Chicago, the day of the martyrs of Chicago, back to El Norte, back to the America which had turned its eyes away from its own past.

And yet, the febrile writer in me couldn't help wandering off into the arcane realm of Bush and the KGB. In an attempt to rid myself of the obsession, I followed up on some of the clues mentioned in that "disappeared" website, struggling to create a thriller that Hitchcock would never have directed, *The Blog Vanishes.*

Or was it *Three Days of the W?*

Either way, a few hours later my cursory search turned out predictably inconclusive.

On May 1st 1973, George W. Bush was supposed to have been in Texas training as a pilot with the National Guard. It is true that there is not one eyewitness that he was in situ during that period. Indeed, not one record places him in Texas or anywhere else during what is known as "George Bush's lost year." So lost is it that the future President did not even report for his physical. Of course, it's more logical to picture him partying, boozing, and smoking marijuana, rather than to conjecture his body being smuggled into some secret Soviet training camp near Uzbekistan or wherever those cloak-and-dagger facilities might have been located, maybe Leningrad. Yes, Leningrad, I thought to myself, now passionately embracing the conspiracy. Leningrad would have been perfect, as that was the one place and time when he might have been offered an early introduction to his counterpart Vladimir Putin, already on his way to his own career in the KGB. It would certainly elucidate one of the most bizarre incidents of all Bush's Presidency, when, at his first (known) meeting with Putin, on June 16, 2001, George W. astonished the world by stating that he had looked his Russian "friend" in the eye and found him trustworthy, that he now had a sense of Putin's soul. And if you look at the video of that encounter, there is a peculiar smile on Putin's lips, perhaps enigmatically reminiscent of Andropov's smile in Red Square all those years ago. Was the Russian President saying to himself, yes, you have a sense of my soul, but I have a sense of your KGB file, my friend, and that probably matters more. You won't utter a peep when I bomb Chechnya.

Enough already. These convoluted ramblings of my imagination would get me nowhere. More relevant was to ask whether the theory of George W. Bush as a KGB agent ultimately made sense of his Presidency. And here, I must admit, reluctantly, that yes, in fact, it did illuminate any number of dark issues that had been puzzling me over the years. Because the truth is that, during his amazingly inept administration, there is only one thing at which Bush had been diabolically efficient and that happened to be the systematic destruction of his own country.

It was easy to understand that as a particularly lethal combination of arrogance and stupidity, laziness and greed. Or it could be interpreted as apocalyptic evangelism run amok. Or we might have focused on the corporations that had him in their pockets or the neocons or…there were so many explanations. None of which really satisfied my desire to grasp how Bush managed to sabotage his own country in such a virulent way. Here was a man who willfully ignored all signs of the terrorist attacks about to be launched on American territory. A man who squandered the goodwill of the world by disastrously invading a country that posed no threat to America's security. Who proved more adept at ravishing foreign lands than rescuing compatriots decimated by a hurricane. Who had bankrupted future generations with his inane tax cut. Who had tried to destroy what was left of his land's social welfare net. Who looked away when people were tortured in the name of America.

It was hard to believe back then that an incompetence so drastic and so persistent was not deliberate. And so, I decided to invent the eccentric website, its mysterious disappearance, the unruly accusations, all of it invented by me as a tongue-in cheek way of using that Mayday landing on the deck of the Abraham

Lincoln to explore and write about what George W. Bush has done to America, where his mission had finally landed us. Because—crazy as my ruminations a decade ago may have been—George W. Bush did indeed act as if he had received secret instructions from some foreign enemy to ruin his land and lay low the American empire, make sure that, no matter what happened to the Soviet Union, it would not be the United States that would inherit the earth.

Crazy back then and yet now, in the midst of the turmoil of the Donald Presidency, now that Russian interference in the U.S. electoral process is no longer a fantasy that I have conjured up as a sad joke, now that probable collusion between Putin and Trump's surrogates is roiling Washington and being investigated by the FBI, now that a Director of that very FBI has been sacked because he would not delay or tone down that investigation, now that international conspiracy and fake websites proliferate, is it not time to ask ourselves if the major question I posed for Bush is not even more relevant for Trump today?

Is he not destroying the very fabric of the American dream, tearing it to pieces shred by shred? Isn't that the mission he is accomplishing, even as he deludes himself and his followers that he is making America Great Again? Acting in the not so hidden interests of all those waiting for America to continue to make the same mistakes that Comrade Bush enacted, but infinitely worse? Is Putin not smiling, somewhat nervously smiling at what he has helped to bring about? Are we not confronted, over and over again, with oligarchs who decide our fate as if we had nothing to say?

And yes, the people, the real victims and perhaps real heroes, are also still here.

We have just lived through another Mayday, with innumerable demonstrators in the streets, protesting primarily against the persecution of immigrants and refugees. Think of this contrast: while Trump proclaimed May 1st 2017 to be "Loyalty Day" (does he have no sense of irony whatsoever?), thousands upon thousands proclaimed their loyalty to a different America that they do not want to see die, a country where "no human being is illegal."

What is paradoxical is that those workers and undocumented immigrants and women who are paid less than their male counterparts, marching though the avenues of Lincoln's country, marching through its hopes and fears and memories, believe more in the promise of America than its President does, no matter that he was born in New York and expresses so lastingly what is deep and permanent in his land.

They are doing more, day and night, to keep this country running and alive than the man who is not, of course, a foreign agent, but, sadly for his fellow countrymen, continues to act more and more like one.

PART THREE

MODELS OF RESISTANCE
FROM THE PAST

12.

MARTIN LUTHER KING MARCHES ON

F<small>ARAWAY</small>, I <small>WAS FARAWAY FROM</small> W<small>ASHINGTON</small> D.C. <small>THAT</small> hot day in August of 1963 when Martin Luther King delivered his famous words from the steps of the Lincoln Memorial, I was faraway in Chile. Twenty-one years old at the time and entangled, like so many of my generation, in the struggle to liberate Latin America, the speech by King that was to influence my life so deeply did not even register with me, I cannot even recall having noticed its existence. What I can remember with ferocious precision, however, is the place and the date, and even the hour, when many years later I had occasion to listen for the first time to those "I have a dream" words, heard that melodious baritone, those incantations, that emotional certainty of victory. I can remember the occasion so clearly because it happened to be the day Martin Luther King was killed, April 4th, 1968, and ever since that day, his dream and his death have been grievously linked, conjoined in my mind then as they are now, fifty-four years later, in my memory.

I recall how I was sitting with my wife Angélica and our one-year-old child Rodrigo, in a living room, high up in the hills of Berkeley, the University town in California where we had arrived barely a week before. Our hosts, an American family that had generously offered us temporary lodgings while our apartment was being readied, had switched on the television and we all solemnly watched the nightly news, probably at seven in the evening, probably Walter Cronkite. And there it was, the murder of Martin Luther King in that Memphis hotel and then came reports of riots all over America and, finally, a long excerpt of his "I have a dream" speech.

It was only then, I think, that I realized, perhaps began to realize, who Martin Luther King had been, what we had lost with his departure from this world, the legend he was already becoming in front of my very eyes. In the years to come, I would often return to that speech and would, on each occasion, hew from its mountain of meanings a different rock upon which to stand and understand the world.

Beyond my amazement at King's eloquence when I first heard him back in 1968, my immediate reaction was not so much to be inspired as to be somber, puzzled, close to despair. After all, the slaying of this man of peace was answered, not by a pledge to persevere in his legacy, but by furious uprisings in the slums of black America, the disenfranchised of America avenging their dead leader by burning down the ghettos where they felt imprisoned and impoverished, using the fire this time to proclaim that the non-violence King had advocated was useless, that the only way to end inequity in this world was through the barrel of a gun, the only way to make the powerful pay attention was to scare the hell out of them.

King's assassination, therefore, savagely brought up yet one more time a question that had bedeviled me and so many other activists in the late sixties and is repeated now in our desolate 2017: what was the best method to achieve radical change? Could we picture a rebellion in the way that Martin Luther King had envisioned it, without drinking from the cup of bitterness and hatred, without treating our adversaries as they treated us? Or does the road into the palace of justice and the bright day of brotherhood inevitably require violence as its companion, violence as the unavoidable midwife of revolution?

These were questions that, back in Chile, I would soon be forced to answer, not in cloudy theoretical musings, but in the day to day reality of hard history, when Salvador Allende was elected President in 1970 and we became the first country that tried to build socialism through peaceful means. Allende's vision of social change, elaborated over decades of struggle and thought, was similar to King's, even though they both came from very different political and cultural origins. Allende, for instance, who was not at all religious, would have not agreed with Martin Luther King that physical force must be met with soul force, but rather with the force of social organizing. At a time when many in Latin America were dazzled by the armed struggle proposed by Fidel Castro and Che Guevara, it was Allende's singular accomplishment to imagine as inextricably connected the two quests of our era, the quest for more democracy and more civil freedoms, on the one hand, and the parallel quest, on the other, for social justice and economic empowerment of the dispossessed of this earth. And it was to be Allende's fate to echo the fate of Martin Luther King, it was Allende's choice to die three years later. Yes, on September 11th, 1973, almost ten years to the day since King's "I have a dream" speech in Washington, Allende chose to die defending his own dream, promising us, in his last speech, that much sooner than later, más temprano que tarde, a day would come when the free men and women of Chile would walk through las amplias alamedas, the great avenues full of trees, towards a better society.

It was in the immediate aftermath of that terrible defeat, as we watched the powerful of Chile impose upon us the terror that we had not wanted to visit upon them, it was then, as our non-violence was met with executions and torture and disappearances, it was only then, after the military coup of 1973, that I first began to seriously commune with Martin Luther King, that his speech on the steps of the Lincoln Memorial came back to haunt and to question me. It was as I headed into an exile that would last for many years that King's voice and message began to filter fully, word by word, into my life.

If ever there was a situation where violence could be justified, after all, it would have been against the junta in Chile. Pinochet and his generals had overthrown a constitutional government and were killing and persecuting citizens whose radical sin had been to imagine a world where you do not need to massacre your opponents in order to allow the waters of justice to flow. And yet, very wisely, almost instinctively, the Chilean resistance embraced a different route: to slowly, resolutely, dangerously, take over the surface of the country, isolating the dictatorship inside and outside our nation, making Chile ungovernable through civil disobedience. Not entirely different from the strategy that the civil rights movement had espoused in the United States. And indeed, I never felt closer to Martin Luther King than during the seventeen years it took us to free Chile of its dictatorship. His words to the militants who thronged to Washington D.C. in 1963, demanding that they not lose faith, resonated with me, comforted my sad heart. He was speaking prophetically to me, to us, when he said: "I am not unmindful that some of you have come here out of great trials and tribulations. Some of you have come fresh from narrow cells." Dr. King was speaking to me and my comrades when he thundered: "Some of you come from areas where your quest for freedom left you battered by the storms of persecution and staggered by the winds of police brutality. You have been the veterans of creative suffering." He understood that more difficult than going to your first protest, was to awaken the next day and go to the next protest and then the next one, the daily grind of small acts that can lead to large and lethal consequences. The dogs and sheriffs of Alabama and Mississippi were alive and well in the streets of Santiago and Valparaiso, and so was the spirit that had encouraged defenseless men and women and children to be mowed down, beaten, bombed, harassed, and yet continue confronting their oppressors with the only weapons available to them: the suffering of their bodies and the conviction that nothing could make them turn back. And just like the blacks in the United States, so in Chile we also sang in the streets of the cities that had been stolen from us. Not spirituals, for every land has its own songs. In Chile we sang, over and over, the "Ode to Joy" from Beethoven's Ninth Symphony, in the hope that a day would come when all men would be brothers.

Why were we singing? To give ourselves courage, of course. But not only that, not only that. In Chile, we sang and stood against the hoses and the tear gas and the truncheons because we knew that somebody else was watching. In this, we also followed in the cunning, media-savvy, footsteps of Martin Luther King: that mismatched confrontation between the police state and the people was being witnessed, photographed, transmitted to other eyes. In the case of the deep South of the United States, the audience was the majority of the American people, while in that other struggle years later, in the deeper South of Chile, the daily spectacle of peaceful men and women being repressed by the agents of terror targeted the national and international forces whose support Pinochet and his dependent third world dictatorship needed in order to survive. The tactic worked, of course, because we understood, as Martin Luther King and Gandhi had before us, that our adversaries could be influenced and shamed by public opinion, could indeed eventually be compelled to relinquish power. That is how segregation was defeated

in the South of the United States, that is how the Chilean people beat Pinochet in a plebiscite in 1988 that led to democracy
in 1990 that is the story of the downfall of tyrannies in Iran and
Poland, Tunisia and the Philippines. Although parallel struggles
for liberation, against the apartheid regime in South Africa or
the homicidal autocracy in Nicaragua or the murderous Khmer
Rouge in Cambodia, also showed how King's premonitory
words of non-violence could not be mechanically applied to every situation.

And what of today? When I return to that speech I first
heard all those years ago, the very day King died, is there a message for me, for us, something that we need to hear again, as if
we were listening to those words for the first time as we confront a danger that would make our hero shudder?

What would Martin Luther King say if he contemplated
what his country has become? If he could see how the terror and
death brought to bear upon New York and Washington on September 11th, 2001, has turned his people into a fearful nation,
ready to stop dreaming, ready to abridge its own freedoms to be
secure? What would he say if he could observe how that fear has
been manipulated to justify the invasion of a foreign land, the
occupation of that land against the will of its own people? What
alternative way would he have advised to be rid of a tyrant like
Saddam Hussein? Would he tell those who oppose these policies inside the United States to stand up and be counted, to
march ahead, to never wallow in the valley of despair? And
Trump! Trump who soils his mouth by quoting Martin Luther

King, Trump, who believes that Frederick Douglass is still alive, who insults the heroic John Lewis as someone who is all talk and no action, mocks John Lewis who was beaten by the police on freedom marches and risked his life, Trump, what would Martin Luther King say to an America that has elected Trump to occupy the office that saw the Civil Rights Bill signed?

It is my belief that he would repeat some of the words he delivered on that faraway day in August of 1963 in the shadow of the statue of Abraham Lincoln, I believe he would declare again his faith in his country and how deeply his dream is rooted in the American dream, that in spite of the difficulties and frustrations of the moment, his dream was still alive and that his nation will rise up and live out the true meaning of its creed: "We hold these truths to be self-evident: that all men are created equal."

Let us hope that he is right. Let us hope and pray, for his sake and our sake, that Martin Luther King's faith in his own country was not misplaced and that more than five decades later enough of his compatriots and mine will once again learn to listen to his fierce and gentle voice calling to them from beyond death and beyond fear, calling on all of us to stand together for freedom and justice in our time.

13.

SEARCHING FOR MANDELA[1]

I T MAY SEEM PARADOXICAL THAT A MEDITATION DEALING
with memory and meant to celebrate the life and legacy of Nelson Mandela should start with the confession that I cannot evoke the date when I first heard his name. When he was imprisoned in 1962, I was twenty years old and an itty bit of a firebrand myself, really of the minor variety, taking time off from my studies at the University of Chile in Santiago to fight the police in the streets and help organize slum dwellers in the shanty-towns of my impoverished nation. South Africa was in our same Southern Hemisphere, and already the symbol of the most unjust and inhumane system in the world, but its struggle was a mere glimmer, resplendent yet distant, on the consciousness of a generation whose heroes were Che Guevara and, closer by, Salvador Al-

---

1 Delivered in Johannesburg on July 31st, 2010. Celebrated each year by the Mandela Foundation to honor Mandela's birthday. I was the first Latin American and the first writer to be invited to speak on this occasion.

lende, who was to become the first socialist elected by democratic means to the Presidency of Chile in 1970. Even during the three years of Allende's peaceful revolution whose ideals could have been modeled on the Freedom Charter of the ANC, even during those thousand days when we did our best to create a country where no child was hungry and no peasant was landless and no foreign corporations owned our soil and our souls, even then, I can't recall that we specifically protested Mandela's captivity, except as part of a general repudiation of apartheid.

It was only after Salvador Allende died in a military coup in 1973, only after I went into exile, when I started to wander this earth like a makwerkwere, that the name of Mandela gradually became a primary beacon of hope, a sort of home to me, now that I was homeless. By the seventies, of course, he had already solidified into a symbol of how our spirit cannot be broken by brutality, but his significance to me also grew out of the collusion of the twin twisted governments that misruled our respective people. The apartheid government that imprisoned him and his fellow patriots and denied them and millions of South Africans their basic rights, turned out to be one of the scant allies of the South American dictatorship that banished me and was ravaging my land. Vorster and Botha were the pals of our Generalissimo, Augusto Pinochet—they exchanged medals and ambassadors and pariah state visits, they sent each other admiring gifts, they shared weapons and intelligence and even tear gas canisters. I could continue with many unfortunate and shameful examples, but one intersection of South African terror and

Chilean terror should suffice: in 1976, the year of the Soweto massacre, we were suffering a slow massacre of our own. The Chilean junta and Pinochet were making infamous around the world the system of disappearing people, arresting them and then denying their bodies to desperate relatives. Both dictatorships sought to create through violence a world where no rebel would dare to step into visibility, would dare to rise up. So my increasing reverence for Mandela in the seventies and eighties cannot be separated from the fact that his people and my people, the people of South Africa and the people of Chile, were bent on a parallel quest for justice against a brotherhood of enemies who wanted to disappear us from the face of the earth, as if our very memory had never existed. Even so, it was not until Chile regained its democracy in 1990 and Mandela's release that very same year, it was not until both his country and mine and indeed the world began to wrestle with the dilemmas of how you confront the terrors of the past without becoming a hostage to the hatred engendered by that past, it was not until both South Africa and Chile were forced to ask themselves the same burning questions about remembrance and dialogue in our similar transitions to democracy, it was only then that Madiba became more than a legend to me and, with his wisdom and pragmatic compassion, grew into a guide for contemporary humanity. Because those of us who had struggled against injustice were to learn that it is often more difficult to listen to your enemies and forgive them than it was to suffer their atrocities, to learn that it may be more morally complicated to navigate the temptations and nuances of freedom than to keep your head high and your heart beating strong in the midst of an oppression that clearly and unambiguously marks the line between right and wrong.

It is these difficulties and these moral intricacies that I would like to explore on this occasion. And I would like to do so from the perspective of a storyteller, someone who, through the decades of battling the dictatorship in Chile, came to believe that he had been spared death many times over so he could keep alive the memory of what the powerful wanted to suppress. Let me start, then, with a story, one that complements and also complicates the story of redemption that Nelson Mandela continues to embody. That is what writers do: plunge into the vast complexity of our human condition rather than be content with simple answers that leave us satisfied and comfortable.

A few years back, while giving away books to schoolchildren in a Chilean shanty-town, as part of a literacy program that an NGO had been organizing, I was approached by an old carpenter. "If it's true that you worked by the side of Salvador Allende," he said, "I have a story to tell you." Carlos—that was his name, if I'm not mistaken—had been an enthusiastic supporter of Salvador Allende's government. Allende had created a program that helped Carlos to purchase his first and only house, Allende had understood why children—including the children of Carlos—should have free milk and lunch at school, Allende had filled that carpenter with hope that workers need not be forever dispossessed of a future, and that this could be done respecting the freedom of all. Following the military takeover of September 11, 1973 that left Allende buried in an unmarked grave and his image forbidden, soldiers raided the carpenter's neighborhood, breaking down doors, beating, arresting, and shooting residents. Terror-stricken, Carlos had hidden away behind the boards of one of the walls of his house a picture of the martyred President, where it remained all through the seventeen years of the dictatorship. He did not extract it, Carlos informed me, even when democracy returned to Chile and Pinochet had to relinquish his stranglehold over the government. Pinochet might not be the country's strongman anymore but he still malingered on as Commander-in-Chief of the Army and his disciples still controlled large enclaves in the judiciary and the media, and, above all, among those who had prospered obscenely during Pinochet's neoliberal regime. Though perhaps more crucially, Pinochet's shadow inhabited the nightmares of many Chileans: they still feared his malevolent aftermath, that he would one day come back and seek revenge. Free elections were not enough to release that carpenter from his dread. The state funeral that Allende received was not enough. And not enough either when a Truth and Reconciliation Commission helped the country come to terms with its past, like its counterpart in South Africa a few years later. It was only in 1998 when General Pinochet, during a visit to London, was arrested for crimes against humanity that Carlos pried back the boards that concealed the portrait of Salvador Allende, and there it was, after 25 years, intact, his *Presidente lindo*, his beautiful President, he said, just as he recalled the man. Taking that portrait from its hiding place changed Carlos. When Pinochet was flown back to Chile after eighteen months of London house arrest, Carlos was scared, but this time he gathered his courage and kept the picture of Allende hanging defiantly on the wall. Never again, he said, was he going to hide it.

It is an inspiring story, because Carlos was not a militant, not a soldier of the revolution sacrificing himself for the common good. That makes his gesture all the more significant. Nelson Mandela has explained how "at the very heart of every oppressive tool developed by the apartheid regime was a determination to control, distort, weaken, and even erase people's memories." Carlos, thousands of miles from South Africa, was rebelling against that very oppressive tool. If that portrait from the past could emerge from its hideout, if it could share the air and mountains of Chile, if he could show it proudly to his grandchildren, it was because Carlos had refused to forget, he had not burned the picture while the security forces rampaged outside but buried it furtively until it could be recovered. If the carpenter could tell me the story at all it was because he had carried that image inside all those outlawed years, nursed and nurtured it.

An inspiring story, yes, but also sobering.

Memory does not exist in a vacuum. If there had been no justice, if Pinochet had not been made to face judges and answer for his crimes during that year and a half in London, the memory of that carpenter would have remained encapsulated. For the memory to flow out into the open the fear also had to flow out, there had to be a societal space where the portrait from the past could be safe. Memory does not exist in a vacuum. The justice that facilitated the surfacing of those proscribed images and thoughts had itself been the product of many other, more public, more communal memories, thousands upon thousands who staked their existence, many of them losing their lives and certainly their livelihoods, so that people like Carlos would not consign their past to the dust of incinerated history, so that people like Carlos would find, when he escaped from his seclusion, a country that was created by voices other than those with more money and more guns. Again, quoting Madiba: "The struggle against apartheid can be typified as the pitting of memory against forgetting. It was in our determination to remember our ancestors, our stories, our values and our dreams that we found comradeship." Carlos was eventually able to bring together his private and his public memory because others risked everything in order for a commons of liberation to exist. For one memory of resistance to persevere it needs, therefore, to eventually belong to a savannah of commonality, it cannot prevail against violence and censorship if it does not join a vast archive of other forbidden memories. The case of that carpenter is sobering, no matter how fervently admirable his loyalty, because the very isolation and secrecy of his hideaway also reveals how ultimately precarious any merely inner and covert rebellion can be.

What if the carpenter Carlos had been killed or exiled or lost his house or perhaps been attacked with Alzheimer's? So many accidents could have blocked that portrait of Salvador Allende from seeing the light. Or worse still, decades hence, someone else, some stranger or maybe even a great-grandchild would have been working on the wall, someone other than Carlos tears out the boards and finds the photo, looks at it wondering why it is there, what unfathomable message it is transmitting from the attic of its mystery? I mention the risks of this further act of forgetting because it seems critical, both in Chile and in South Africa, to urgently ask ourselves how we are to transmit the memory of struggle and resistance, sorrow and hope, to the young, how to transfer something more than a piece of paper, a scrap of celluloid, how to transfer the most elusive thing that needs to be handed on to the next generation: experience. Experience: what it meant to live under apartheid in South Africa, what it meant to survive tyranny in Chile. The photo that the carpenter hid away thus becomes a metaphor for both the endurance of memory and its inevitable state of flux. The photo as an object may be there but the carpenter who once suffered to keep that memory alive will pass. Memory does not exist in a vacuum. Unless it becomes active in the lives of the young, relevant in the lives of the young, it will die as surely as it would have if the security forces had torched the carpenter's house.

Time, alas, is on the side of death and oblivion.

Nor is relentless time the only problem faced by those who struggle against forgetting. A series of questions about reconciliation percolate from the carpenter's story. How to reconcile—and I use the word purposefully—how to reconcile the memory of that carpenter with the memory of the men who would burn that photo of Allende, would burn the body and eyes and hands of the man who would remember Allende, how to reconcile his memory with the contrary and powerful and menacing memory of the men who would burn the very shack in which that man lives, burn down the country that is desperate to bring that memory into the open? Enemies remember the past differently. Until they agree in some way on that past, and are able to forge a memory common to both sides, their rivalry will refuse to vanish. That is why Truth and Reconciliation Commissions, with all their flaws and concessions, all the pain they do not expose and all the crimes that may remain unpunished, are an indispensable step in a transition to democracy after a period of systemic violence. These inquiries create a version of history that the majority of citizens and especially their children can access, a story that becomes the inexorable frame of reference for future dialogue and discussions. The narrative in which former adversaries can concur gradually turns into the narrative of the nation itself, a form of collective memory that can persevere beyond the life of its original protagonists, even as we acknowledge that this consensual story far too often leaves out too much of the grief, too many recalcitrant stories, and should be understood as the beginning of a process and not its end.

Because this creation of a shared history through the public airing of a harsh past does not unavoidably lead to true reconciliation. Other steps may be necessary to heal a divided community. Other steps may be needed to reach those who refuse to accept how their own actions have offended our common humanity. Other steps may be vital if we are to keep the past alive for future generations.

Let me revert again to a story, another tale of disputed recollection and even more disputed reconciliation, but more disturbing than the fable of the carpenter and his clandestine portrait of Allende.

I happened to be in Chile in 2006 filming a documentary based on my life, when our nemesis General Pinochet was hospitalized for a heart attack, a stroke from which he would die one week later. I first warily circled to the back of the Hospital Militar where Pinochet was being treated and as I talked to a group of journalists, a woman passed by and insulted me, calling me a dirty communist. I responded with intensity but not aggressively: "Why are you attacking me, ma'am? What have I said or done?" She didn't answer, swishing away around the corner to the front of the hospital. And there they were, outside the gates of the medical facilities, a group of women, crying out for their dying leader, led by a small, chubby woman, lips thick with lipstick, fingers clutching a portrait of her hero, a litany of tears streaming from behind incongruous dark glasses. There she was, making a pathetic spectacle of herself for all the world to see, defending a man who had been indicted by courts abroad and in Santiago as a torturer, a murderer, a liar, and a thief. And yet, I was paradoxically, inexplicably, uncontrollably moved by her misery. And so, unable to stop myself, I approached the woman, told her how I had mourned Allende and therefore understood that it was now her turn to mourn her leader—but also wanted her to realize how much pain there was on our side.

This sequence of the film is the one that, particularly in Latin America, calls forth the most criticism. How, people ask, could you do that? How could you validate that woman's grief for Pinochet, honor it as similar to your grief for Allende? How could I extend my sympathy to an enemy who was condoning the misdeeds of Pinochet, had probably celebrated that someone like me was tortured or exiled or executed by her dying hero? What possessed me? That's what people keep asking.

That's the right word. In effect, I found myself *possessed*. I was inexplicably, uncontrollably moved by that woman's misery, unable to hold myself back, as if some deep turmoil or angel inside had welled up and overwhelmed me.

Psychologists have discovered that a baby will cry more intensely and for a longer period of time when she hears the distressed cries of other children than if the doctor conducting the clinical trial plays back the baby's own sobbing voice. Think about it: a baby is more upset by the voice of someone else's agony than by her own troubles. The baby intensifies the cries in solidarity with the other, shares the pain, signals to the other child that she is not alone. For me, this is proof, if we ever required it, that compassion is ingrained in our species, coded inside the circuits of our brain. This is how we managed to become human, by creating the conditions for a social network where the suffering of others is intolerable, where we need to pity and comfort the afflicted. It is certainly not the only thing that defines us as humans: we are also characterized by cruelty and selfishness, indifference and avarice, but each of us can decide what defines our primordial humanity, and I choose the pre-eminence of empathy with others as our most important trait, the base for our evolution. What lays the groundwork for our search for language is the articulation and belief that someone else will accompany us through life. Compassion is at the origin of our species-quest for the imagination with which we can smuggle ourselves into and under alien skin. What possessed me, then, was quite simple: I felt sorry for that woman.

And yet, we also ought to interrogate my act. That hysterical woman, after all, rants against those who have "mala memoria," literally, "bad memories," targeting precisely people like that carpenter Carlos who remembers Allende and refuses to forget the crimes of the General. It is her memory against ours and there is nothing I can do in this world—or doubtless in the next one—to change what she recalls, what she has selected to recall in order to defend the identity she has built for herself. Her narrative, her most intimate story, the myth by which she has lived for decades, is that Allende was a socialist who threatened her peace and property, so if Allende's followers were put violently in their place by the substitute father Pinochet it was in order to save that woman and her family from the hordes, to protect her from the barbarians. She starts from the same paranoia as that other woman in the film who, when I first arrive at the back of the hospital, insults me as she strides away, calling me a dirty communist. With this major difference: the mournful woman holding the portrait of Pinochet is willing to listen, is able to at least have a face to face encounter with me, recognizes me as a fellow human, perhaps because I approached her with gentleness and respect, perhaps because I broke down her preconceptions about the enemy. It's hard to open a dialogue with a harridan who slurs invective and then shows us her back. But when her ally, that other woman who was wailing, ceased her tirade, I saw a crack in the barrier she had erected and ventured into the potential breech to tell her that though we disagreed on fundamentals, I could still understand her distress. In return, I asked that she try to put herself in my shoes, realize that I was not afflicted by a "mala memoria," bad memories, but merely memories that did not coincide with hers, that might, in fact, be antagonistic to hers, but that this was not a reason to kill or detest one another.

Before that encounter, I had meditated extensively in my plays and novels on the walls that separate us from those who have done us grievous harm, I have compelled my characters to deal with their worst enemies and ask themselves how to avoid the sweet trap of victimhood and retribution. I had suggested that atonement was essential for any significant exchange of ideas to transpire, essential that he who had benefited from a transgression give up his privileges as proof that he was sincere. But when it came to real life I could not wait eternally for that repentance. In real life, I felt the urge, if only for a minute, to break down those walls myself, to leap across the divide, to imagine a different sort of world.

I was not offering reconciliation and most definitely not for-giveness to that Pinochetista fanatic. For a long-term ceasefire to exist some remorse would have had to bite inside, she would have had to be willing to inhabit my memories, to accept what Carlos the carpenter had been through during twenty-five years trying to keep alive his own river of memory in the midst of the conflagration. I would want her to recognize his right to show his portrait publicly, as she does, without fear. I would want her to acknowledge his right to exist, our right to mourn, our right to remember. She is undeniably very far from that state of grace. But we did create, she and I, some minimal space for a minimal understanding, a gentle interlude—and, as South Africa proves, those truces when ardent foes begin to speak to each other can be the start of something miraculous. You do not arrive at such armistices effortlessly, you often need to drive your opponents to the table through force and cunning, you cannot suppose that such meetings of the mind will simply happen—each small step is fraught with peril and false enticements and perverse illu-sions. Let me repeat this: each photo, each memory, does not emerge from its hiding place without struggle and suffering, without an immense social movement behind it, without some form of justice enacted.

It is also true, however, that far too frequently those magical instances when adversaries meet and reach at least a pact not to resort to carnage to impose their points of view close just as abruptly as they open and we often find ourselves yanked back to where we began. I can shatter that wall, open a splinter in time and reside there for the snap of a minute, but there will be no further progress unless the other side, people like that woman who insulted me, people like the woman who is closeted in her anguish over the impending death of a tyrant, like the soldiers who raided the shanty-towns in Chile, like those who profited from the suffering in South Africa, manage to take a step of their own, realizing that to admit their own complicity in these crimes is a way of liberating themselves from their own prison of prejudice and hatred.

As South Africa has proven, it is not impossible to make exceptional encounters like the one with that woman last longer than a minute, to become part of a country's major reckoning with itself.

In 1997, on my first, and up till now only visit to your country, I was taken to District Six in Cape Town, that site of conscience that commemorates what happened in a multiethnic neighbourhood torn apart by discrimination. As I toured the museum with one of its guardians, he told me about a recent hearing of the Truth and Reconciliation Commission. A policeman of Afrikaner origin admitted killing the parents of a child and expressed regret for his actions. When the grandmother of the boy asked him what would happen when she was dead, who would care for this orphan, the policeman had answered, after a pause: "Then I guess I will have to take the child home with me."

It is a wondrous story. So perfect, in fact, that as soon as I was invited to deliver this Lecture, I decided to make use of it here this afternoon. And in order to give that chronicle more historical heftiness, I tried to track it down through my friends at the Mandela Foundation, but in spite of assiduous research, no concrete reference was uncovered. Nor could curators from the District Six Museum evoke the anecdote nor could several journalists and writers. It was always the same answer: nobody could summon up that story. I cannot, therefore, offer a name now, or put flesh and blood on the protagonists.

Ultimately, however, it may not matter if such a policeman and such a grandmother factually exist, if one said this or the other said that in exactly the way it was recounted to me, it may not matter if my guide at the District Six Museum had heard a garbled version of the tale and then retransmitted it in a different form, because that is how memory often works. Communities give themselves the chronicles they need in order to understand the world just as individuals create for themselves the stories they need in order to survive with a sense of self. If a story is true in its core, if it tells us a higher truth, something unforgettable about ourselves, then it remains true even if it is partly invented.

Or can anyone deny that the policeman was expressing a model of behavior, was informing the grandmother and the eavesdropping world beyond her, that policeman is telling us all here, right now, today, that we cannot undo the damage of the past but must strive instead to undo the damage to the future, we must prove in our actions tomorrow that we have learned from the terrors and sins of yesteryear? What other way to pay for the taking of the lives of a mother and a father than to bring back home the child whom you orphaned, what other way to pay for a life taken than to give a life back?

It is probable that such a homecoming envisaged by the policeman cannot occur in reality: before a black orphan would be brought into the house of the oppressor, many others in his own community would care for that boy. But as a metaphor, as epic drama, as a pluri-cultural ideal, what more could we ask for, what better challenge to present day South Africa, what better image of a multiracial omni-linguistic home can be offered? Is that policeman not speaking across continents and time to the woman who cried for Pinochet, is he not demanding that she take Carlos the carpenter home with her? Is he not affirming that it is his duty, as a policeman, to protect the carpenter's portrait of Allende, his right to display that portrait on the wall, rather than persecuting him for his memories and his ideas? Are we not all being invited to bring into our homes what is concealed behind the walls of our identity, that which most disturbs us, those memories from the thickets of others that we have considered to be alien, to be hazardous to our integrity? Is it not in that back and forth process of offering a refuge to those who are different that we can find intimations of what it means to reconcile or at least move down a pale path towards tolerance? Is this not what literature and art do incessantly, invite us into the homes of strangers so we may know ourselves better, create a startling birthplace of common language from which we can explore an enigmatic world?

Above all, however, I would like to concentrate on the homeless orphan and what it might mean to him to be taken care of, to be truly cared for. Because all my words are meaningless unless they reach that child, unless they help fashion a world which that child deserves to inherit, unless the stories I have been telling speak to that boy who has lost his elders. I wonder, in fact, if that child, now grown, is not listening or watching this lecture, if he will not come forward in the days ahead to claim his public place, emerging from the hazy boundaries of storytelling into the history of his country, like the photo of Allende yearned to emerge into the history of my own land.

Think of children like him, boys like him, girls like him, all over the world. Think of them as potentially homeless because of our actions. We may not have murdered their parents, but we have built societies where girls and boys from every latitude and climate are in danger: famines, sicknesses, war, drought, poverty, beatings, pollution, civil strife, refugees and xenophobia, drugs and ignorance, women deprived of their rights, the compassion of the world's religions hijacked by fundamentalists, leaders who seem to have no control over events, high officials of governments tolerating thuggery and corruption when they should know better, are not all of these crimes against humanity and the future? Worse still, there may be no future: we still have nuclear weapons that can render ourselves and our brother and sister animals extinct, we have blindly allowed our planet to be plundered and desecrated by our greed and our desires and our indifference. How can we take the child back home with us if there is no earth itself to greet him, no home for us all? What message of hope do my three intertwined stories deliver to those children and to a world crying out for concrete solutions to dire dilemmas?

Memory matters. One of the primary reasons behind the extraordinary crisis humanity finds itself in is due to the exclusion of billions of human beings and what they remember, men and women who are not even a faraway flicker on the nightly news, on the screen of reality. One of the ways out of our predicament is to multiply the areas of participation, to create veritable oceans of participation. To offer room and respect to those memories and stories is not a merely charitable, paternalistic initiative, but an act of supreme self-preservation. A nation that does not take into account the multitude of suppressed memories of the majority of its people will always be weak, basing its survival on the exclusion of dissent and otherness. Those whose lives are not valued, not given narrative dignity, cannot really be part of the solution to the abiding problems of our times. We cannot afford to wait twenty-five years, like that carpenter did, for each hidden dream to step into the light of day.

For that light to come, we must discover ways to diminish the fear that seeps into every aspect of our contemporary condition. The fear that we will be punished if we raise our voices. The fear that we will be mocked or derided if we reach out to those with whom we disagree. The fear that our attempt to redress the wrongs we may have committed will be met with rage and the desire for revenge.

Fear, yes, fear is our real enemy and its main victim is always trust.

That may be the central plea of this lecture: that if we do not trust one another, we shall all die.

It will not be easy. Unless we recognize the need for all the hidden photos and memories of the poorest and most neglected on this earth to find a safe haven, there will be no trust. There will be no trust unless we make efforts to disarm the most powerful, those who believe themselves the exclusive owners of the truth and can therefore, when they are challenged, commit all manner of crimes and misdemeanors in the name of their apprehension. And perhaps we need to start by disarming our own selves, admitting that none among us is so perfect or saintly that we are immune from the temptations of power and dominance, perhaps we should try to conquer the fear of our own nakedness. And then, maybe, who knows, others will trust us.

Can it be done in time? Can we take the children home with us? Before we destroy our planet?

Let us attend then to the message of hope that Nelson Mandela has been sending us.

One of the major pleasures of Madiba during his captivity was his garden. He tells us often of how uplifting it was to plant and harvest under the sun and rain, to be in control of that small patch of earth when he controlled nothing else in the world except his dignity and his memories and the certainty that his comrades would continue struggling. He tells us of the joy of sharing with his fellow prisoners but also with his jailers the bounty that his labors produced, what he and the land birthed into existence in spite of the injustice and the sorrow and the separations.

Mandela's garden is not a fluke, an exception. Recently I have been reading a book called *Defiant Gardens*, by Kenneth Helphand, who recounts the story of gardens created improbably in the midst of the viciousness of war. The desperate gardens of the Warsaw Ghetto and the stone gardens cultivated by the Japanese Americans in their internment camps during the Second World War, the vegetable beds fashioned in the shadow of the trenches of the First World War, the gardens which flourished minimally, at first hesitantly, then insolently, and always with gentleness, as the bombs fell in Vietnam and as American soldiers prepared to fight in Korea and the Persian Gulf. What is fascinating about this array of landscapes is that these diverse and divergent gardeners do not align themselves on the same side in war; they might even be sworn enemies. And yet, they are all human, they all hunger for flowers and fruit, they all ache to keep alive a hint that something will grow in spite of the surrounding night of destruction.

There is no guarantee that we will ever reach the deep reconciliation we need as a species. Indeed, I tend to think—it may be the transgressive writer in me—that some damage done is irreparable. I notice that when justice comes infrequently the most long-lasting memories are in danger of fading. But when despair visits me, I hold on to the image of the garden. A garden that grows like memories should. A garden that grows as justice should. A garden that grows like true reconciliation should.

And do not forget that for crops and vegetables, for leaves and trees, to grow, we need to sing to them.

We need to sing to the earth so it will forgive us and continue to provide hope.

We need to always remember the multiple, infinite gardens of Nelson Mandela and his people.

14.

THE TRUTH THAT MADE HER FREE

ARLY ON THE MORNING OF DEC. 3, 1980, A FARMER ON A remote road in El Salvador spotted four bodies lying in a ditch. It was a sight that had become inexcusably normal, even unexceptional, in that small "breathtakingly poor" Central American country in the throes of a civil war and a guerrilla insurrection. That year alone, over 8,000 men, women and children had been slaughtered, most of them by the government's armed forces and paramilitary death squads.

Once the corpses were identified, however, it turned out that there was indeed something exceptional about these particular victims. Not that all four were women, not that two had been raped, not that the perpetrators did not care to hide their crime. What made this into an international scandal was that the women happened to be United States citizens rather than "ordinary" Salvadorans, and that three of them, Ita Ford, Dorothy

Kazel, and Maura Clarke, were Catholic nuns (the fourth, Jean Donovan, was a lay volunteer doing missionary work).

Eileen Markey's *A Radical Faith: The Assassination of Sister Maura*, just published at the end of this terrible 2016, is not an investigation into the killing itself, like Francisco Goldman's *The Art of Political Murder*, a masterly book that delved into the web of intrigue and deception surrounding the 1998 homicide of Bishop Juan Gerardi in Guatemala. But what Markey accomplishes is something equally valuable: to painstakingly map out the path that brought one of the nuns, Maura Clarke, who was nearly 50 years old, almost inevitably to that ditch in a foreign land.

Tracing Maura's roots to a patriotic Bronx childhood suffused with religious imagery and brimming with stories about her immigrant father's dedication to the cause of Irish independence, the author explains why the Maryknoll order was a natural home for someone who cared so lovingly for others and wanted to alleviate their pain. Markey also explores Maura's own doubts about her worthiness for such a vocation. The story, a bit ponderous at the beginning, at least for this nonreligious reviewer, picks up once Maura arrives in Nicaragua in 1959 and gets involved with the needs and hopes of her parishioners. It then accelerates even more dramatically once the community she had come to worship as the living embodiment of Jesus joined the Sandinista insurgency destined to topple the corrupt and tyrannical Somoza regime. The final chapters chart Maura's experience in El Salvador after she answered, not without some trepidation, the call by

Archbishop Romero (himself assassinated during Mass a few months before her own death) for Maryknoll sisters to assist the church at a moment when its children, the peasants, and the squatters of his country, were being persecuted in ways reminiscent of early Christians under the Roman Empire.

Her final months of activism—ferrying refugees out of conflict zones, offering sanctuary to survivors of massacres, transporting food and medical supplies to faraway and wounded communities, documenting atrocities in case prosecution might someday be viable—resonated with me personally. At the time, in 1980, my wife and I lived in exile from our native Chile, where a similar resistance was growing against General Augusto Pinochet's dictatorship. And just as members of the clergy in Chile were targeted by the military authorities for their part in the struggle, so too were the churchwomen in El Salvador targeted for defending the human rights of people they saw as "blessed temples of the Lord."

Maura and her colleagues chose to ignore the death threats they began to receive, insisting that the Good Shepherd does not abandon the flock to the wolves. And so it was that the wolves descended upon them, their broken and mutilated bodies meant to be a lesson in fear. If even American nuns could be killed with impunity, who then was safe?

Eileen Markey has meticulously researched the many fluctuations of her subject's journey, visiting each place Maura inhabited, parsing government cables and memos, combing through thousands of private letters, interviewing scores of men and women whose lives were touched by the martyred nun, with no fact, factor, or marginal event left unreported. I sympathize with this passionate urge to help the dead speak, to rescue a voice of love that has been silenced forever by violence. And yet, that exhaustive zeal can also be somewhat, well, exhausting. Do we really need to learn about the trips of Maura's innumerable relatives, or that "being home was delicious" and be immediately reminded in the same paragraph that "it was heaven to be home"? Surely it's unnecessary to reiterate every few pages that Maura had a beautiful smile, conveying all over again how open, conciliatory, and friendly she was? I could go on with other instances where some judicious editing would have been welcome, but none of these minor limitations make the book any less important.

Because this is not only the story of one woman. It personifies a movement, a generation, an era in history. The old-fashioned church that Maura entered, that preached obedience and submission, changed after the 1962-65 Second Vatican Council and the Medellín bishops' conference of 1968, opening the door to a fiery theology of liberation. The nuns now felt compelled to denounce "the hierarchies that condemned so many people…to poverty" and to demand that the church itself, conservative and male-dominated, examine its own role in the unequal distribution of wealth and power. For many who served in religious orders—and Maura is a shining example—this new understanding of the Gospel meant siding with revolution against dictatorship, even at the risk of sharing the fate of a God of the poor who had died on the cross. And, in the case of Maura and many of her religious co-workers, it also meant realizing that her country, the United States, was aiding and abetting the very tyrannies that kept el pueblo de Dios in bondage. Her critique of American foreign policy and Cold War complicity in war crimes is made all the more striking when one considers that the officer who led the death squad that executed her and another who gave the orders had been trained at the School of the Americas, an institution run by the United States that continues to this day to "educate" the military of Latin America despite persistent calls to shut it down.

At a time when many in Maura's country are once more questioning its imperial role in the world and her church is yet again searching its soul for ways to save not only the forgotten of the earth but the earth itself, this nun's life and sacrifice seems more relevant than ever.

Of the many scenes from that life, one of the last ones may be the most moving and memorable. The night before Maura was murdered, she wrote to her ailing parents in the United States: "The human family will always search and yearn for liberation." And added the words: "I'll call you soon."

She never got to make that call. But "A Radical Faith" has resurrected her so that Sister Maura can, in fact, call out, and continue her mission in search of justice. There is no better time to listen to this brave, compassionate woman, a committed role model for all those who, secular or religious, want to be "truly free."

15.

READING CERVANTES IN CAPTIVITY

O F THE MANY TIMES THAT, SINCE ADOLESCENCE, I HAVE returned to *Don Quixote de la Mancha*, there is one which, archetypical and collective and unique, I choose to remember, that I cannot help but remember. That reading, more than forty years ago, along with a desperate group of captive men and women, matters singularly when the commemoration of the 400th anniversary of the death of Miguel de Cervantes compels us to ask if that seminal author, besides the delight and pleasure he affords us, has an urgent message for our turbulent twenty-first century.

Cervantes in person could not have imagined a stranger, more diverse, more appropriate gathering of readers of his book if he had resurrected with that sole purpose than those who were jam-packed into one of the ample salons of the Argentine Embassy in Santiago, sometime in mid-October of 1973. Outside that building, death stalked the city. A month before, on September 11th, the military had overthrown our President, Salvador Allende, and a reign of terror had begun against the people of Chile.

I had spent the month since the coup living clandestinely, barely one step ahead of General Pinochet's secret police, until the Resistance ordered me to seek asylum in the Argentine Embassy. Once I had managed to smuggle myself past the soldiers who surrounded the premises, I was greeted by almost a thousand men, women, and children raggedly camped out in rooms meant to receive a few honored guests for cocktail parties. It was a hellish scene: a once-opulent garden obliterated by trampling feet. Malodourous bodies lined up endlessly in front of bathrooms that were broken from overuse. Everybody was perpetually hungry, as the kitchen was too small to prepare meals for so many ravenous mouths. And, above all, there was an overwhelming sense of suffocation, above all the stench of desolation and fear.

Reading *Don Quixote* was part of a plan to combat that depressing atmosphere during the long weeks ahead, as we awaited safe-conduct that the Military Junta was loath to grant. Having taught that novel at the University, I had volunteered to lead an expedition into its depths, anticipating that the boisterous escapades of the Ingenious Hidalgo and his squire Sancho Panza would serve as an antidote to anguish and grief. Might we not all extract hope, and more than some flickers of laughter, from a hero who persistently roams the roads of Spain in search of widows to defend and orphans to champion, undeterred by the blows that rain down upon him because he insanely tries to re-vive the ideals of chivalry that his society no longer values?

That dose of good cheer first required obtaining a copy of the book, and the fascistic Argentine functionary, the First Secretary of the Embassy in charge of the unwelcome boarders, a tall, jowly, unpleasant man whose name I definitely prefer not to remember, was dismissive of my request. He commented, deri-sively, that we should have read that novel before embarking on our doomed attempt to radically change society. "You tilted at the capitalist windmills," he sneered, "and the windmills gave you a well-deserved beating, not that your kind will ever learn anything other than running like rats."

In spite of such invective, that official, perhaps grateful that we had not demanded bomb making manuals or the diaries of Che Guevara, ended up delivering into my hands a copy of *Don Quixote* that was soon warming the hearts of thirty some refu-gees who had up until then been in touch only sporadically, and always superficially, with that Cervantes novel. Besides a few Chileans, most of these improvised readers had come to our country from the failed revolutions of other Latin American lands—Uruguay, Bolivia, El Salvador, Colombia, Guatemala, Brazil, and, of course, Argentina. They therefore brought to the book a wealth of maturity and experience, and a depth of vul-nerability and mourning, that had been lacking among my young University students. Many of these militants had been locked away for prolonged periods of time, had suffered torture and oppression and exile, had tried to keep alive inside the caverns of defeat and sorrow and loss, a thirst for justice that Cervantes would, I am sure, have sympathized with, even if a writer of his era (despite admiration for More's *Utopia*) could hardly have been expected to espouse the same socialist principles. Like them, Cervantes had been the victim of astonishing adversity, and also like them, was challenged, as he wrote the two parts of *Don Quixote*, to stay immensely resourceful in a cruel and disenchanted world.

Indeed, the defining experience of our Miguel's life, what made him into the man and artist he was to become, were the harrowing five years (1575-1580) that he spent in the dungeons of Algiers as a prisoner of the Berber pirates. It was there, on the border where Islam and the West clashed and mixed, that Cervantes learned to value tolerance towards those who are radically different, and also there that he discovered that, of all the goods that men can aspire to, freedom is by far the greatest. While awaiting a ransom that his family could not pay, confronted with execution each time he valiantly attempted to escape, watching his fellow slaves tormented and impaled, he longed for a life without despotic walls or manacles that bound him to an arbitrary master. But once he returned to Spain, a crippled war veteran neglected by those who had sent him into conflict, once he found himself jobless and without recognition, as disappointments and betrayals piled up, he came to the conclusion that if we cannot determine the misfortunes that assail our bodies, we can, however, hold sway over how we react to them, we can engage in the more crucial task of emancipating our soul.

Don Quixote derives from that revelation. In the prologue to the First Part of his novel (1605) he tells the "idle reader" that it was "begotten in a prison, where every discomfort has its place and every sad sound makes its home." Given that Cervantes was jailed many times in his life, always unfairly, always persecuted by corrupt and inept magistrates, we do not know for sure which Spanish city deserves the bizarre honor of housing the prison where the initial, tentative glimmers of the Ingenious Hidalgo first saw the light, but what seems certain is that this new traumatic experience of incarceration, which forced him to revisit the Algerian ordeal, thrust him face to face with a dilemma that he resolved to our joy: either succumb to the bitterness of despair or let loose the wings of his imagination, prove that we humans contain within us a limitless, indeed divine, capacity to go beyond the immediate materialistic prison-house of this Earth. The result, eventually, was a book which would push the frontiers of creativity, unfettering his writing from the chains and boundaries of previous literature, subverting every tradition and convention Cervantes had inherited. A miracle: instead of a rancorous indictment of a decaying Spain that had rejected and censored him, Cervantes invented a tour de force as playful and ironic as it was multifaceted, laying the ground for all the wild experiments in uncertainty that the novelistic genre was to undergo over the centuries, a fountain from which every writer since has been drinking.

Hailed initially for its farcical, festive, entertainment value, readers over the centuries gradually came to recognize that they were living, suffering, performing in the multidimensional windmill grind of everyday existence that Cervantes, for the first time in Western history, had proclaimed as worthy of fascinating, deliberate, caring narration. He realized, with tender brutality, that we are all madmen constantly outpaced by history, fragile humans powered by the mirage of who we are and what we desire, imprisoned by an identity built out of how others view us, shackled to bodies that are doomed to eat and sleep, to defecate and make love and someday die, made ridiculous and also glorious by the figments and ideals we harbor. Cervantes, to put it bluntly, discovered the vast psychological and social territory of the ambiguous modern condition. Captives of a harsh and unyielding reality, we are also simultaneously graced by the constant attempt to surpass, with some semblance of dignity, its battering blows. It was the genius of Cervantes to gently force his readers to concede and then jubilantly celebrate that they were equally woven out of the fabric of both Don Quixote and Sancho Panza, that his two supposedly opposite heroes are, in effect, indispensable components of one hybrid humanity seeking freedom.

Those of us reading *Don Quixote* in 1973 in an Embassy we could not leave, surrounded by troops ready to transport us to stadiums and cellars and cemeteries, responded viscerally to that riotous work conceived in circumstances not dissimilar to those we were enduring. That continuous exaltation and practice of liberty, both personal and aesthetic, was inspiring, the wager that, beset though we may be by the most sordid events and accidents, we are all, each last one of us, a magnificent, ongoing experiment that only ceases with our final breath. This faith that the human spirit cannot be crushed was epitomized by a passage from the Second Part of *Don Quixote* that moved us to tears.

Sancho Panza has been made governor of a fictitious *insula*, an Isle, by a Duke and his lady, keen to amuse themselves at the expense of their guests. The lowly squire proves to be a far wiser and more compassionate ruler than the noblemen who mock him and his master. One night, doing the rounds, he comes upon a young lad who is running away from a constable. The boy gets cheeky with Sancho and the erstwhile governor sends him to sleep in prison. Infuriatingly, the prisoner insists that he can be put in irons and chains but that no one has the power to make him sleep, that staying awake or not depends on his own volition and not on the commands of anyone else. Chastened by this example of independence and self-possession, Sancho lets him go.

It is an episode that has stayed with me ever since. If I call it to mind again now, it is because I feel it contains the essential message Cervantes still has for today's desperate humanity.

True, most of the planet's inhabitants are not in prison, like Cervantes so often was, nor do they find themselves confined, like the revolutionaries in the Argentine Embassy, by multiple walls of dread. And yet we live, more even than the author of *Don Quixote*, in a world rampant with shifting mirrors and mirages, ever farther from one another, a species captured by violence and inequality, greed and stupidity, intolerance and xenophobia, marooned on a planet spinning out of control. As if we were lunatics sleepwalking towards the abyss.

Cervantes died four hundred years ago and yet he continues to send us words, the wisdom transmitted by that boy threatened by Sancho Panza, words that we need to read again and listen to and meditate upon before it is too late.

Nobody has the power to make us sleep if we don't wish it ourselves.

Cervantes is telling us that our besieged, besotted, captive humanity should not lose hope that we can awaken in time.

16.

THE DANCING COSMOS
OF ALBERT EINSTEIN

INSTEIN WAS SUPPOSED TO BE THE GENIUS OF EYES AND light.

But it turns out that ears listening in the dark to the hidden music of the universe are his last gift to us. I am not surprised. As a child, I was sure that Albert Einstein was the most famous violinist in the world.

The confusion stemmed from a photo of the great man that adorned the New York *Times* in the late 1940s—let's say 1948, to conveniently and coincidentally make me six years old, the very age when Einstein himself, in 1885, first started his violin lessons. That morning of 1948, my father opened the paper in our home in Queens, New York, and pointed to the man with the bushy moustache and wild hair and gentle laughing eyes. "The greatest man of our time," my father informed me solemnly. "And I met him several times, when I was at Princeton in 1944, at the Institute of Advanced Studies. He even invited me to his house, served me tea. And how he played the violin!"

And that was enough, the awe with which my father pronounced those words *he played the violin*, for me to believe for many years that the most eminent physicist in history was renowned primarily for his ability to coax notes out of a musical instrument.

In time, of course—oh, yes, in time—I came to realize the errors of my ways. He began to appear on my horizon when my adolescent brain staggered to understand that mass and energy can be manifestations of the same phenomenon and then loomed even larger as my adult brain began to pen stories where the distinction between past, present and future is only a stubbornly persistent illusion full of curves. And appeared in all his metaphorical glory when, growing older in a globe defined by what Einstein had discovered, a century torn asunder by the forces that this wonderful man had unleashed, I found my life splintered as if it were an atom. And through it all, I also came to admire Einstein as a man of peace and wisdom and yes, a prankster—with that renowned tongue of his sticking out at us from his most notorious photograph and demanding that we not take him—or ourselves—all that seriously.

So many images, so much influence, the unforgettable speed of light in the center of the galaxies, and ever less my original impression of Einstein as a musician.

And yet, now that we are learning, with amazement and

humbleness, that the universe is filled with the gravitational waves that Einstein predicted as existent in 1916, just over one hundred years ago, now that the ears and not the eyes of humanity will chart the inside of black holes and beyond, I have started to wonder if my first intuition about the great Albert was not correct after all. I wonder if those early violin lessons in 1885— for a boy who had not yet started to really enunciate words, who was a tardy speaker of German—were not the sweet fire where his mind was forged and tempered. If it was not in the mass of that wooden musical instrument filled with a baffling energy that resonated inside every electron of his being, if it was not there where and when and how he first conjured up the laws of cosmology. I wonder if the design of the universe was not contained in the emotion he wrested from those strings. And if it was not a heart tuned by Mozart that gave birth to his certainty that the quantum leap of the imagination is always more important than the dreary accumulation of conventional knowledge. Can it not be my final wonderment—that Einstein's grand cosmic theory owes more to an aesthetic revelation than to his overwhelming mathematical intelligence? That he surmised his gravitational waves of the great beyond from the waving, weaving sounds in the intimacy of his brain?

Because this he did know, really knew—and said it: "We all dance to a mysterious tune, intoned in the distance by an invisible piper." And was exceptional because he understood this mystery, that distance, this invisibility, that piper, in a deeper and more humane way than most of those who, full of uncertainty and bewilderment, have danced ever since in the still luminous shadow of his music and his mind.

Isn't it time—again, time!—that we listen to him all over again, now that refugees like him are denied safe passage and haven, now that the science that he defended with a fierce intelligence is under siege, being derided and underfunded, now that the hate crimes and anti-Semitism and discrimination of the sort he and his fellows suffered are rampant and retweeted by so many in power, isn't it the moment to celebrate the melody of the messages that he, like a distant, pulsating star, is still sending us?

Here's to you, Uncle Albert—the greatest violinist in the world.

17.

REVISITING MELVILLE IN CHILE

ANTIAGO DE CHILE MAY SEEM A STRANGE PLACE FROM which to try to understand Donald Trump and how to resist his most aberrant edicts and policies, and yet, it is from the distance and serenity of this Southern Cone city, where my wife and I live part of the year, that I have found myself meditating on these issues, abetted by the insight and doubts of none other than Herman Melville.

When the Pinochet dictatorship forced me and my family into exile after the 1973 coup, the vast library we had laboriously built over the years (with funds we could scarcely spare) stayed behind. Part of it was lost or stolen, another part damaged by a flood, but a considerable part was salvaged when we went back to Chile after democracy was restored in 1990. What strikes me about these books that have withstood water and theft and tyranny is how they enchantingly return me to the person I once was, the person I dreamt I would be, the young man who wanted to devour the universe by gorging on volume after volume of fiction, philosophy, science, history, poetry, plays. Simultaneously, of course, those texts, mostly classic and canonical, force me to measure how much desolate and wise time has passed since my first experience with them, how much I myself have changed, along with the wide world I traveled during our decades of banishment, a change that becomes manifest as soon as I pick up any of those primal books and reread it from the inevitable perspective of today.

It is a happy coincidence that the works I have chosen to revisit on this occasion are by Melville, as I can think of no other American author who can so inform the perilous moment we are currently living. Roaming my eyes on shelf after shelf, I soon lit upon his enigmatic novel *The Confidence-Man: His Masquerade*, and sandwiched between it and *Moby-Dick*, a collection of his three novellas, *Benito Cereno*, *Bartleby, the Scrivener*, and *Billy Budd, Sailor*.

Having just participated, as an American citizen, in the recent election that elevated to the presidency an archetypal liar and devious impostor who has hoodwinked and mesmerized his way into power, *The Confidence-Man* seemed like an appropriate place to start. Though published 160 years ago, on April Fool's Day, 1857, Melville could have been presciently forecasting today's America when he imagined his country as a Mississippi steamer (ironically called the *Fidèle*) filled with "a flock of fools, under this captain of fools, in this ship of fools!"

The passengers of that boat are systematically bilked by a

devilish protagonist who constantly shifts his identity, changing names and shape and schemes, while each successive ambiguous incarnation tries out one scam after another, swindles and snake-oil-trickery that were recognizable in his day—and, alas, in ours. Fraudulent real estate deals and bankruptcies, spurious lies disguised as moralistic truths, grandiose charitable undertakings that never materialize, financial hustles and deceptions, bombastic appeals to the honesty of the suckers while showing no honor whatsoever—it all sounds like a primer for Trump and his buffoonish 21st-century antics and "truthful hyperbole." Of course, Melville's time was not the age of Twitter and Instagram and short attention spans, so his ever-fluctuating rascal engages in endless metaphysical discussions about mankind, quoting Plato, Tacitus, and St. Augustine, along with many a book that Trump has probably never even heard of. And rather than a bully and a braggart, this 19th-century pretender is garrulous and genial. But just like Trump, he displays an arsenal of false premises and promises to dazzle and befuddle his victims with absurd and inconsistent projects that seem workable until, that is, they are more closely examined—and then, when cornered by demands that he provide proof of his ventures, the scamp somehow manages to distract his audience and squirm away. And also like Trump, he exercises on his dupes "the power of persuasive fascination, the power of holding another creature by the button of the eye," which allows him to mercilessly best his many antagonists, exploiting their ignorance, naïveté, and, above all, greed.

Indeed, Melville's misanthropic allegory often seems less a denunciation of the glib and slippery trickster than a bitter indictment of those gullible enough to let themselves be cheated. The author saw the United States, diseased with false innocence and a ravenous desire for getting rich, heading toward Apocalypse—specifically, the Civil War that was a scant four years away. Fearful that, behind the masquerade of virtue and godliness performed by the role-playing passengers, there lurked shadows of darkness and malignancy, he was intent on revealing how the excessive "confidence" in America's integrity, virtuousness, and "ardently bright view of life" can lead to tragedy.

And the novel ends in a quietly terrifying way. As the light of the last lamp expires and a sick old man, one final quarry of the Confidence Man, is "kindly" led toward extinction, the narrator leaves us with this disturbing forecast: "Something further may follow of this Masquerade."

Those words pester me, because the "something further" that we are living today is a grievous circumstance that Melville could not have anticipated: what if somebody like the slick Confidence Man were to take power, become the captain of that ship of fools—in other words, what if someone, through his ability to delude vast contingents, were to assume control of the republic and, like mad Ahab, pursue the object of his hatred into the depths (in Trump's sea there are many white whales and quite a few minor fish) and doom us all to drown along with him?

If Melville was not concerned with the possibility that his Confidence Man might become a demented, uncivil president, he did bequeath us, nevertheless, three short masterpieces where the protagonists rebel, each in their own special way, against an inhumane and oppressive system. By reading once again the novellas *Bartleby*, *Billy Budd*, and *Benito Cereno*, I hoped, therefore, to discover what guidance Melville might provide to those of us who ponder how to fight the authoritarian proclivities that Trump and his gang epitomize as they seek total and uncontested power to radically remake America.

I began, obviously, with *Bartleby, the Scrivener*.

"I would prefer not to": those are the emblematic words with which the protagonist, a copyist for a Wall Street lawyer (who is also the bewildered narrator of the tale), invariably responds when asked to perform the most minimal tasks but also when offered a chance to better or protect himself, to the point of losing his job, his housing, and, eventually, his life, as he ends up starving his body to death in prison. When I initially read this novella in my youth, I saw it, not incorrectly, as an allegory about Melville himself. At the time of its writing—in 1856, a year before the experimental, uncompromising *The Confidence-Man* was published—the author (whose *Moby-Dick* had sold poorly and been, in general, misunderstood when it appeared in 1851) was struggling with his own refusal to accommodate his style and vision to the commercial literature of his age, a refusal that corresponded with my own 1960s ideas about not selling out to the "establishment." Though I was able to grasp, as many readers have since *Bartleby* appeared, that this radical rejection of the status quo went far beyond a defense of artistic freedom, delving into mankind's existential loneliness in a Godless universe, it is only now, beleaguered with the multiple dangers and dilemmas that Trump's authoritarianism poses, that I can fully appraise the potential political dimensions of Bartleby's embrace of negativity as a weapon of resistance.

Not because his ascetic withdrawal, passivity, and "pallid hopelessness" are what the majority of Americans who voted against Trump need in these times of bellicose regression. It is, rather, the specific way in which the protagonist posits his rebellion that may serve as a model for those of us who feel threatened by the aggressiveness of this president, who, like Ahab, is "possessed by all the fallen angels." What disarms, indeed what leaves Bartleby's employer "unmanned," is that the scrivener's responses are unwaveringly mild, "with no uneasiness, anger, impatience or impertinence." Bartleby's individual intransigence was insufficient to change the disheartening world in Melville's time, but it is a great place from where to start an active resistance in ours.

Imagine "I would prefer not to" as a rallying cry. Sanctuary cities and churches: "I would prefer not to help hunt down undocumented men, women and children." Indigenous tribes and veterans and activists: "I would prefer not to step aside when the tanks and the pipelines roll in." Civil servants at federal agencies: "I would prefer not to enact orders to destroy the environment, eviscerate the public school system, deregulate the banks, devastate the arts, attack the press; I would prefer not to cooperate with unjust, misguided, stupid, contradictory executive orders; I would prefer not to remain silent when I witness illegal acts that violate the Constitution," and on and on we could go, on and on we must go, if we are to be free. If every opponent of Trump were to adopt this stubborn and placid refusal to go along—each deed of collective defiance always begins with somebody individually saying "No!"—our belligerent president would find it difficult to impose his will, though we should expect a great deal of pressure against and persecution of those who stand in his way. Indeed, there are far too many signs already that dissidence, criticism, recalcitrance, whistleblowing, and protests will be met with the full force of the state.

Whether such repression manages to control those who challenge Trump on multiple levels will not only depend on the obduracy and cunning of the president's adversaries, but also on how the judiciary intervenes in this battle. How justice is served and, indeed, interpreted, will determine whether the orders of a fraudulent occupier of the executive branch can be contained.

It was thus natural to plunge next into the most distressing of Melville's works, the last one he ever wrote (it remained unfinished at his death in 1891), the haunting and haunted *Billy Budd*. The title character is a sailor, conscripted into the British navy, who never thinks of using the words "I would prefer not to," but, on the contrary, is agreeable and compliant. An angelic being, almost divinely handsome, able to lighten each day's burden with his good cheer, popular among the crew and the officers, Baby Budd, as he is called, is an innocent lamb of a man loved by everybody on board the *Bellipotent*. Well, not everybody—precisely this wholesome harmlessness and beauty creates in Claggart, the master-at-arms of the ship, a hatred, rage, and envy, an "unreciprocated malice," that Melville attributes to sheer depravity and unfathomable evil. Given that Claggart is in charge of policing, discipline, and surveillance, he has at his disposal an arsenal of means to trap Billy, deceitfully accusing him of conspiring in a mutiny, at a time when the British Navy had been wracked with widespread revolts by sailors. When confronted with this indictment, Billy—afflicted by a "convulsed tongue-tie" incapacity to speak out when he is under extreme emotional stress—responds by striking Claggart. The blow kills the satanic master-at-arms—and Billy must face trial in front of a hastily convened drumhead court.

The administration (or mismanagement) of justice that follows is the crux (I use the word deliberately, as we will witness a crucifixion) of the story. Melville goes out of his way to praise

Captain Vere, the commander of the ship: he is well-read, fair, brave, often dreamy, eminently honorable, and has a sincere fatherly affection for Billy Budd, intending to promote him. And he does not doubt that Claggart (for whom he feels "a repellent distaste") is lying, nor that his victim knows of any conspiracy or harbors a single mutinous thought, and yet, Vere's reaction to the homicide is peremptory:

"He vehemently exclaimed, 'Struck dead by an angel of God! Yet the angel must hang!'"

Having thus passed judgment on Billy Budd, Vere will manipulate his court of junior officers (all dependent on him and under his authority) to declare the sailor guilty, without allowing for palliating circumstances or for the matter to be referred, as naval practice and law demand, to the admiral for adjudication. In order to get the verdict he desires—fearing that compassion and flexibility might encourage disorder and sedition—he must ignore his private conscience and yield to the imperial code of war and argue against a "warm heart," which he calls "the feminine in man" and thus must be distrusted and "ruled out." This failure of the father figure to protect the weak is a tragedy not only for Captain Vere himself (who will die in battle not long after this incident, with Billy Budd's name on his lips as he agonizes) and for the blameless handsome sailor (who dies blessing the captain who has wronged him), but for humanity itself in its journey toward redemption.

If Melville is concerned with the miscarriage of justice (and one can only hope that the US courts will differ from Captain Vere by shielding those who are unable to defend themselves from malignant attacks and overreach by the government), his novella also probes another disquieting matter that obsessed him all through his life: the question and legitimacy of violence.

Violence comes in many guises and varieties in *Billy Budd*. There is, of course, the violence of the state, which Captain Vere incarnates and exercises with "full force of arms." And then there is the violence of Claggart, the official enforcer of order who abuses his power and becomes an instrument of perfidy and immorality. But most interesting is Billy Budd himself. Why does the angel deliver the lethal blow that will annihilate him? He speaks with his fists when his tongue and throat are struck dumb by an assault upon the core of his being so wicked that he could not foretell it. Indeed, it is his extreme good nature, his unwillingness to recognize evil—despite having been warned that Claggart, with "his small weasel eyes," is out to get him—that leaves him unprepared. One could almost venture that our ill-fated hero has too much trust and "confidence" in his fellows.

Melville had already explored these issues of innocence and violence in *Moby-Dick*—where the crew and officers are unable to stop the crazed skipper of the *Pequod* from driving them all to ruination (all, that is, save the narrator, who wants to be called Ishmael)—but it can be argued that nowhere did he delve deeper into those predicaments than in *Benito Cereno*, serialized in a magazine in 1855 and revised when it was published as part of *Piazza Tales* in 1856 (again, just before *The Confidence-Man* appeared).

This traumatic story is centered on an astounding event at sea that actually happened, as I vaguely recalled as I opened the book, off the coast of southern Chile, a few hundred miles from where I was now re reading it. A group of slaves—the year was 1805—took over a Spanish vessel, killed most of its white crew and passengers, and demanded that the captain, Benito Cereno, return them to Africa. Melville moves the date to 1799 and re-baptizes the ship the *San Dominick* in order to more closely parallel the successful and extremely ferocious—slave insurrection against the French on the isle of Saint-Domingue that would lead to the establishment of Haiti, the first black republic in the world. He is basically saying to his unheeding American public: this bloodletting awaits us if we do not end slavery.

What is extraordinary about *Benito Cereno* is that Melville has chosen to oppose slavery not by staging, as in *Uncle Tom's Cabin* or so many abolitionist tracts and memoirs of the day, the cruelty and viciousness of those who hold other humans in bondage but rather by dramatizing how, when those slaves seek liberation through the only fierce means available to them, they will imitate their masters, use the same fear and torment that was imposed upon them to make sure that their former overlords do not dare to rebel. But that is not all: Melville presents this dire reversal of roles through the eyes of Amasa Delano, a well-meaning and decent American captain who, having generously sailed to the rescue, is duped by the masquerade that the slaves have forced the surviving whites on board to perform: that the ship has succumbed to a series of misfortunes (hurricanes, illnesses, adverse winds), that have left most of the whites on board dead and most of the blacks alive and wandering the deck helplessly, the eternal social order intact. Filled with racial prejudices, Delano is unable to conceive that not only have the slaves broken out of what he considers their natural state of submission and submissiveness but that they have the subtlety and intelligence to create such an intricate plot. His blindness to the possibility of evil (the evil that is slavery and how that evil can also infect the slaves themselves) derives from his blindness to his own complicity in that evil, his failure to distinguish shadows from light, appearance from reality.

Amasa Delano joins a long list of Melville's male protagonists (there is hardly a spirit-lifting woman or a child in his bleak tales) who are contaminated by innocence, who do not understand that, as a character in *The Confidence-Man* says, "nobody knows who anybody is" in a world that is a "painted décor," where the worst of us hide their vilest appetites and sins under a veneer of nobility and the best of us are oblivious to the depths and spirals of that villainy. Melville's heroes can be fooled because they are fooling themselves. It is the case of Billy Budd, who does not wish to even consider what Claggart is up to. It is the Wall Street lawyer, oblivious to how his style of life and aspirations are ultimately responsible for Bartleby's refusal to cooperate. It is Benito Cereno, who never realized that the cargo of slaves he was carrying could spell his doom. It is Captain

Vere, who suppresses the feminine in his heart in favor of the law of war without realizing that a few days later he will die in that war, that he has killed himself by hanging Billy. It is the case of the predestined company of the *Pequod*. There is no dearth of tenderness or affection, no lack of humor and intimations of hope in Melville's parables—and he glories in the wonders of storytelling—but his basic message to America (and the world) is to wake up.

Reading these cautionary chronicles in the light of today's disastrous Trump ascendancy, what struck me most was how so many Americans were unmindful, as Melville's characters are, as to what the future would bring, the collective incapacity (and I include many of Trump's supporters) to imagine, like Billy Budd, that such malice and trickery exist. And I admit that I shared the presumption that there were enough decent and good-willed white people in the United States to stop the lowest moral citizen in the land from capturing the highest political office, the most powerful office on the planet. A sin of optimism: America is too good, too exceptional, too wonderful a country to commit that sort of fatal mistake.

Risky as it may be to extrapolate and extract prophetic words about the future from an author long dead, I might warrant that Melville would thunder: you fools. Fools, those who believed and continue to believe in Trump despite all evidence that he has conned you. And fools, those who thought it could not happen here and did not fully measure the rage and inhumanity blighting America since its inception. And more fools, all of you, to think it might get better than worse as the deranged days rush by, deluding yourselves that the institutions that have provided checks and balances through so many calamities will stand this test.

Wake up. Claggart is plotting and waiting in the wings. A dictatorship is far from impossible.

If it's any consolation, America is not alone in its blindness.

I started re-reading Melville in Chile animated by the expectation that my distance from the United States would help me to see how this author could illuminate the America of today and tomorrow, but to my surprise, as I advanced into his fictional universes, I had to admit that the frailties he was exposing and the quandaries he was scrutinizing could be applied to the country where my reading was taking place, a country whose long struggle for equality and justice, culminating in the peaceful 1970 revolution of Salvador Allende, had been sadistically suppressed.

Chileans back then nursed the illusion that our democracy was stable and enduring, only to be inconsolably awakened by the military coup of 1973, becoming aware, when it was too late, of the fragility of our institutions. How quickly so many of our people succumbed to demagoguery and brutality, how easily they normalized the everyday malice of dictatorship as they fell under the spell of consumerism.

But I also recognized in Melville's masterpieces the very forms of resistance that many of us contemplated during those seventeen years of tyranny. Confronted with regression, shattered by grief, abandoned by the judges who were too craven and cowardly to defy the despotism of General Pinochet and his oligarchical civilian acolytes, we had to choose between the armed rebellion of the slaves on the *San Dominick* or the "I would prefer not to" of Bartleby. Though there were some—a small group—among the military's challengers who embraced violence against such a nefarious regime as righteous and the only path to victory, the enormous majority of the democratic opposition were wary of this insurrectionary strategy. It was a tactic destined to fail, we thought—and we were wary of the consequences of that violence, even in the unlikely case that it could be successful rather than counterproductive. History had taught us the same lesson that Melville had presaged in *Benito Cereno*: far too often have the revolutionaries of today become the oppressors of tomorrow, repeating the mistakes and coercion of yesterday. And so, with the infinite patience of an Ishmael and the insubordination of a Bartleby and the angelic resolution of a Billy Budd, we vanquished the Claggarts of Chile.

Would the American people be able to do something similar?

Melville might say, I presume, that it cannot be done without a drastic ethical transformation of the country, the recognition that Trump is the mere excrescence of America's dark soul. Our author would point out that what now plagues us are the sins of the past coming home to roost: America's tolerance of bigotry and racism, America's optimistic blindness to its own faults, America's love affair with bogus spectacle and masquerades, America's culpable innocence amid imperial expansion. The Confidence Man—and Men—will continue to triumph until the citizens—or enough of them—take responsibility for having helped to create a land where Trump's victory was not only feasible but, at some point, almost inevitable, a nation where so many Americans felt so alienated and abandoned that they willingly embarked on the "ship of fools."

Of course, Melville wrote at a time when the submerged voices of humanity were hardly able to make themselves heard. So many of his protagonists are either rendered speechless in moments of crisis, like Billy Budd, or remain mute, like the slaves on the *San Dominick*, while their story is told and twisted by someone else, someone more powerful. Even Bartleby cannot rationalize or articulate why he rebels. And, except for the narrator, none of the sailors and officers of the multiethnic *Pequod* survive to tell the tale of the White Whale. Melville saw his blasphemous literature as providing an alternate version to the official "truth" of dominant history.

Today things are different. The voices of those who will and must engage in civil disobedience are anything but silent as they try to avoid the impending catastrophe.

And so, when I wonder if Melville's fellow countrymen and women will be able to withstand the onslaught of the Confidence Man's presidency, when I ask myself if the best of the

American people will find the strength and cunning to force those in power to listen, when I try to imagine what sort of land the future holds, I leave the answer to that great ally of ours from the past, our eternal Melville. Here is how I prefer—yes, prefer—to envision that tomorrow where "something further may follow of this Masquerade," describing it with some magical words culled from *Moby-Dick:* "It is not down in any map: true places never are."

Or better still: "I try all things, I achieve what I can."

PART FOUR

WHAT IS TO BE DONE?

18.

HOMELAND SECURITY ATE MY SPEECH[1]

DEAR MADAME PRESIDENT OF THE MLA, WITH GREETINGS to my fellow panelists and audience members:

Last night, at dinner, when you informed me that Julia Kristeva was not going to participate in our Presidential Forum due to health problems in her family, I must confess that, along with sadness at her absence, I found myself wondering whether this unfortunate circumstance might not allow me to save myself some embarrassment by reading out her speech instead of mine. But you had already asked someone else to do so and I find myself, therefore, unable to cover for the fact that I cannot deliver the words I had prepared for today's plenary session. Something unexpected happened yesterday, unexpected and yet

1 The speech in question was part of a plenary session of the Modern Language Association (MLA). I do not feel comfortable, for reasons that will soon become obvious, disclosing the date or location of that speech, which was addressed to the President of the MLA who had invited me to be one of the four panelists.

perhaps not unforseen. Please believe me that this is not your typical THE DOG ATE MY HOMEWORK excuse with which all of you in this audience of university professors are undoubtedly familiar.

This really happened.

Yesterday, upon my arrival from Latin America at Miami International Airport, at exactly 10:31 in the morning, two agents from the Department of Homeland Security impounded my speech on "The Role of the Intellectual in the Twenty-First Century."

You might think that such things cannot happen in the United States. And indeed, you have the right to remain skepti-cal. In fact, that was one of the points in my speech: that we have not only the right, but the obligation to remain skeptical. And rebellious. And vigilant. The only right we do not have is the right to remain silent.

But I am getting ahead of myself.

The point is that the batteries in my computer ran out almost as soon as the plane took off from Caracas—maybe that's why they stopped me, because I was coming from insubordinate, both-ersome, chaotic Venezuela—and I made the mistake of spending the flight handwriting my speech, presuming that all fifteen pages would be easily transcribed once I had landed. But history is full of "I wish this" and "I wish that." I could wish, for instance, that I had the total recall memory of Funes el Memorioso, that charac-ter in a story by Borges who did not know what a computer was, that I hadn't been selected to step aside for what those men swore was a random check, that I had never watched my bags being ripped opened and every document and paper scrutinized. What would Funes el Memorioso have done if he had been forced to answer questions by two intimidating agents of homeland security? But then, he probably wouldn't have minded if they kidnapped his speech to the MLA because all he would have had to do to retrieve it was dip into the endless archive of his memory.

But not me. I can't recollect the exact details of what I wrote and my lawyers, working in conjunction with legal counsel from the ACLU and the journal *Possession* which was supposed to publish my remarks, have declared that it will take at least five years of judicial maneuvering to recuperate my manuscript, so that does leave me with the dilemma of what to do with my allotted time today. Given that the Kristeva gambit did not work, I contemplated the possibility of skipping ahead today to what every audience member really loves in any presentation, the juicy give and take of the q and a, but there is not supposed to be a question and answer period today and, besides, how can you ask questions about a speech I haven't delivered? I considered the Nabokovian option of making up the questions and the answers, but no, better to simply describe to you what transpired between myself and those agents in that room where the portrait of Donald J. Trump glowered down at me from the wall in a rather foreboding way. I hesitate to call it a conversation, I dare not call it an interrogation, let's just say it was a vigorous and frank discussion of the speech they held in their hands, particularly as it pertained to the new President and the so-called war on terror and the aftermath of September 11th 2001, what I called "the other September 11th."

Which is what may have got me into trouble. What do you mean, "so-called"?, the agents kept asking, perusing the words with which I had started the speech I was never to deliver. What do you mean, that you cannot focus on the terrorist attacks on New York without linking them to this other remote and far-away and neglected September 11th in 1973, when Chile was devastated by a military coup? Does it mean, they asked, well, one of them, the shorter, stockier, beefier one asked, does it mean, he asked, that Chileans might be seeking retribution, revenge maybe, for the role the United States presumably had in the overthrow of the Allende government? Was I planning some act of aggression, nursed for more than forty years? Did I know anything about Chilean sleeper cells that would awaken now that Donald J. Trump occupied the White House?

No, I answered, in regards to revenge, my whole position was precisely the opposite. I explained that we Chileans had been victims, we had been attacked and we had not answered the violence inflicted on us with a surge of violence against the foreign power that had intervened in our democracy, we had not used terror against terror, had not imitated our aggressors. Here was a model, therefore, of how suffering can make you mature, I said, help you ask the right questions and maybe arrive at the right answers, no matter how tentative. And I repeated that word: tentative, as if it were a life saver, something to hold onto in that overly lit, overheated room.

They seemed to be listening to me quite assiduously and that's when I thought to myself, hey, I can argue with them, I can talk them through this, that's what I am, that's what I'm supposed to be, someone who argues and remonstrates and reasons, believes in reason and scientifically proven facts—isn't this what we're here for, isn't this the true role of the intellectual—or at least one of the possible roles—to convince the uninitiated? Hadn't I written somewhere in my lost speech that the most formidable intellectual challenge of our era is not how to reach out yet one more time to the thousands who admire Susan Sontag but to connect instead with the immense audience that watched Celebrity Apprentice or the sixty-five million Americans who read the apocalyptic *Left Behind* series? Not that the two quite modest and self effacing security agents looked as though they thought of themselves as worthy of appearing on a reality TV show nor believed, for that matter, in an imminent rapture that would end history and devour the unbelievers but, like any two bored bureaucrats, they seemed intent instead on devouring the good hot lunch that I was keeping them from.

Nevertheless, I sensed that this was a golden opportunity, here was praxis rather than theory, precisely what the left has been preaching we need to do in the age of Trump, reach across the blue-red divide. Here were two functionaries in all their glorious subalternity and marginality, people we never heard from in literary conventions, and they had read my speech not once but twice, and seemed furthermore willing to thrash out my ideas with me! Talk about q and a! I had uttered that word, tentative, which I somehow recalled as being central to my sequestered speech, so I decided to immediately address that issue, see if I could persuade my guards that to be tentative and nuanced is crucial at this moment in history, the need for uncertainty and ambiguity and philosophical insubordination, I told them, at a time when we are being fed official lies as if they were facts and facts as if there were an alternative to them and fake news as a way of ignoring the real news, and all the more important, therefore, to show ourselves humble to our adversaries, accept the insecurity of our own doubts, I said, warming to the subject, instead of the false security of complacency, the false—

The other agent interrupted me. "All right, all right, you've made your point." He was taller and a bit gangly and more academic looking with his Trotsky-like glasses perched on his nose, and I wondered whether they had been told not to play the tired game of good cop/bad cop, been instructed to perform the roles of academic cop versus vulgar cop, nerd versus bully. Maybe they were a team that had been specially trained to weed out suspicious aliens with scholarly leanings and post-modern inclinations, maybe that's where all our billions of tax dollars had been going, maybe they were smart enough to realize that I was absolutely harmless, so harmless that they could even give me back the speech. But did I really want to seem that harmless? Wasn't that a way of accepting my own ineffectuality, admitting that it didn't really matter at all what I wrote, what I proclaimed, what the whole MLA did or did not do, regardless of the rantings of Ann Coulter or Steve Bannon's anti-elite tirades? Typical petit bourgeois angst: do we want to be dangerous and persecuted or do we want to be aloof and left alone? Are we members of a community or do we thrive on independence of opinion?

The brainy agent didn't leave me much time to cogitate about this dilemma.

"We're at war," he said. "You know what wars are like. According to this speech of yours you were once in a life and death struggle to get rid of a dictator, and when you were in the midst of that, I don't think you were so enthusiastic about ambiguity and tentativeness and nuance. This General Augusto What's His Face was bad, you were good—didn't you at that point embrace an inflexible position? Or were you full of cute intellectual fluffiness back then, maybe this, maybe that, maybe something else? Were you like that during the Allende years, when you were besieged by your enemies?"

He had a point. I have to admit this Homeland Security Agent with his Kansas accent had scored a point. I appealed to his sense of fair play.

"There's no easy answer to that," I said. "If you'll just give me some minutes…" As the tall agent did not seem to object, I plunged on, trying to ignore his partner who was lolling back in his chair disrespectfully, picking his teeth with what seemed to be a—could it be a matchstick? "There are times," I continued, and the words somehow sounded a bit hollow and artificial in that windowless room in the Miami Airport. Hadn't I sworn to avoid manifestos, hadn't I written in that very speech that we need to be wary of anything that smacks of preaching? But I was already swimming in my own words and there was nothing to do but keep at it. "There are times," I went on, "when everyone is tested, times of national emergencies or even of world emergencies, when each person feels that life and death hang in the balance—their lives, what they believe in, the fate of the planet itself, all of it, hanging in the balance."

"What?" interjected the beefier man, chewing the words as if they were another matchstick. "You believe in global warming? Another one who's fallen for that hoax crafted by the Chinese so we'll stop growing industrially and they can become Número Uno?"

"Hey, let him finish his thoughts," his colleague said. "We're not here to examine climate change. We're here to determine if his speech needs to change, that's our job: to do some extreme vetting of his words, understand if they pose some sort of danger to our national security, right, and we can't do that unless we let him talk, right? So, you were saying something I happen to agree with, and our President believes as well, that there are perilous moments in our history…"

"Yes," I took up the slack, "and those moments may shake intellectuals more than anyone else, because in an age of trouble and confusion, to think well suddenly seems to matter more than before, to understand the nature of the crisis we are facing may be a real contribution to ending that crisis, there may be no more important task than to find a strategy to communicate that quest for understanding to one's fellow citizens. You've had those moments in your own history," I said to those Homeland

Security gents, "here in the United States, just before the Civil War, during the Depression, in the Sixties—when the turmoil was so immense that many artists and intellectuals felt the need to grapple with and engage in the vital issues of their day. We're at one of those moments now. You gentlemen may not agree with me on what needs to be done, but at least we agree that the Republic faces clear and present danger."

"So what makes you so special?" demanded the beefier man. "How come you know the answer?"

"I don't. I have no idea what the answer is. I just happen to have some experiences that I have been struggling with for a long time, you know, searching for those answers. And those moments in my past, I had hoped they were somehow exemplary, might serve as a sort of guide for us in our current predicament, could be used to define the role of the intellectual, what's in that speech which you have illegally seized."

"Listen, Professor—you don't mind if we call you Professor, do you?"

"You can call me Professor all you want, though I'm now retired."

"You don't look retired. You look obsessed. But anyway, Professor, retired or whatever, so tell us the formula, the gist of it, as you're so hot on communicating to your fellow citizens. In one sentence, what is the role of the intellectual in the twenty-first century? In twenty-one words or less, Professor. One for each century."

And the other one, the brainy one, added, "You're so interested in history? You know what Ike, President Eisenhower that is, called an intellectual? A man who takes more words than he needs to tell more than he knows. So give it to us in twenty-one words or less. And if you manage not to be excessively long-winded, you know what? We'll let you go."

I took a deep breath and started. I told them that there may not be a clear-cut definition, that perhaps we can't safely speak of THE role of THE intellectual, as if there were only one. Rather, there are many different levels of intellectual activity, a multitude of often contradictory options. Because intellectuals react differently, as Edward Said once made clear, according to the historical circumstances they happen to find themselves in, that's what I told them.

And that's also when I stopped. I wondered whether quoting Said was wise, they probably thought he was Muslim and not of Christian birth if they even knew who he was, which I very much doubted, but they might know he had been born in Palestine, and they might start asking me my views on Netanyahu or maybe from there they'd veer to Iran and the enthusiasm for Rumi that I had expressed on NPR, who could tell what dossier about me they had compiled, and anyway I was way over my allotted quota of twenty-one words and at this rate would soon be closing in on twenty-one thousand. They wouldn't fathom what I was talking about, they were hundreds of sound bite miles away from what I was saying, where I was coming from, the abyss between us was increasing with every word I uttered.

How to express in a formula what it had meant to feel life

quicken and explode in the revolutionary Chile of Salvador Allende, when the underclass of a nation was fighting to express itself and take control of its destiny, and everything around me was bursting to find words and colors and thoughts that had never before been given a chance to emerge in our history? And how would these agents take it if I said that the present moment, right now in 2017, though far from revolutionary, was overflowing with energy and hope, the widespread resistance conjured up by a First Bully more imperious and imperial than any in the already violent past, so many movements, so many causes, so many unforeseen hurricanes and tempests of people, maybe even neighbors of these two agents, people who were struggling for a new language, were breaking out of the conventional strait jacket of politics? And that it was a matter of learning how to dream again. What would these agents say if I suggested intellectuals had to learn how to dream again? But if I said that, I would have to add that we also had to be careful not to allow the dreams to fly unfettered into the wild, that we needed to subject the dreams to scrutiny, that the critique of the enthusiasm was as important as the enthusiasm itself, that this was something I had learned and might come in handy in the years ahead. Because defeat also teaches you something. And then when democracy returned to Chile in 1990, victory also taught us something. That even in that delicate moment, when the military threatened to come back to power if we rocked the boat and were too critical, even at that risky moment, and above all at that moment, it was crucial to brutally question who we were, where we were going, why we were going there. Brutally crucial to be transgressive, especially in victory. But perhaps most valuable of all my experiences, most valid for the hazardous twenty-first century was what had happened to us after the coup of 1973. It was a dire situation and all the more dire because we were unprepared for it, we had not readied ourselves for what was coming. Most of the Chilean elite and the Chilean people themselves had never before lived under the shadow of such a ferocious dictatorship. On September 10th of 1973 we had been free to express ourselves, had books and newspapers and radios and TV stations and streets at our disposal and on September 12th we were being hunted down, arrested, executed, tortured, banished, forbidden. What mattered, of course, at first, was to survive—but survival is not enough, survival is never enough if you wish to change the world and not merely suffer it. So the years that followed forced intellectuals into many activities: at times nothing more than to denounce and offer information, fight amnesia, tell the truth as simply as possible. Because one true word is worth ten thousand lies, we have to believe that one true word is worth more than a million lies. And that was something to remember for today, for 2017, and for tomorrow.

For tomorrow, that is, if the planet and the species survived.

But I needed to be optimistic, to recall that there were other things we had done from exile and from clandestinity and from resistance: bear witness, for instance, offer a space for stories and voices to grow. And analyze, never stop trying to understand the new circumstances in which we found ourselves. And care for the word, care above all for the contaminated words, the words that had been deviated and abused and mal-appropriated by power, the words that we would have to nurse and heal and rescue if our children were ever to speak freely in a free land, carry the right vocabulary through the turmoil so that something survived the onslaught of mendacity and mediocrity and fear. Yes, fear. To be fearless, maybe that was the formula, that was the simple phrase I could furnish to these two homeland security agents.

But would they understand? Fear, they would snort, You're afraid? Here in the United States? Just because we stopped you at random and read your stupid speech twice and are asking you some routine questions? You really think this is like Chile in 1973? You think we Americans have anything to learn about dictatorship, here, when you are free to leave as soon as we've chatted with you a bit, free to scurry off and make remarks at the MLA or the PMLA or the MLAPK or Muslim Liberation Alliance, or whatever it's called?

And I knew that if we began to talk about the parallels between Chile and the US, well, then the discussion would get really entangled. I would have to explain the deadly process that had been crawling out of the swamp of September 11, 2001, the menace of what lay ahead, how sadly familiar the current state of affairs was to me, the renditions, the torture, the eavesdropping, even disappearances—desaparecidos here in the United States! —the imperial presidency, the secrecy and corruption, the cowed and submissive press, the inane justification of pre-emptive violence, the lies, the simplification of ideas, the degradation of discourse, the militarization of society, the fear, the fear.

And how all that had led, ultimately, despite Obama, perhaps because of Obama, as a reaction to the perceived menace of Obama, to Trump. And the nerdy agent would smirk at me, accuse me of simplifying when I had promised nuance, could I seriously accuse Trump of creating a police state, of emulating Pinochet? Was I going to throw around words like fascist without scrutinizing the clear historical differences?

And I would have to admit that, in effect, we don't live in a police state, not yet, not yet, but who could deny that the same doctrine of national security which poisoned Chile is taking over every inch of public space and every corner of public dialogue, who could deny that all it would take was a really devastating attack, an act of colossal terror, for the landscape to change even more drastically, for democracy to founder, and then yes, I could well find myself back in this room and it wouldn't be so easy to get out next time, it wouldn't be a casual conversation next time. It could happen here, it can happen anywhere, that is what I needed to say, that is what I did not say. I did not say that we Chileans had indeed learned lessons of some value during the long years of repression and terror and banishment, discoveries also made by so many others in the precarious nations of the world. I did not say that now was specifically the time when an exchange of ideas and experiences across time and geography and cultures was required, now was the time to examine how remote intellectuals had sought to surmount the catastrophe which had befallen them in their forgotten lands, now was the time to remember how we had managed to think ourselves out of that catastrophe.

Think ourselves out of a catastrophe.

Not a bad formula. Isn't that precisely what defines an intellectual in times of strife, in this present moment of adversity and also in the future as more disasters loom; isn't that the best way to use our talents, our knowledge, our imagination, our intelligence in the twenty-first century?

So I formulated it to them: "Here are my twenty-one words. Count them: We're living a catastrophe and need to find ways to think ourselves out of it, think ourselves out of the catastrophe."

The brainy one counted the words with pursed lips and nodded; his associate stood up from his chair.

"All right, you go and do that, Professor, go do some thinking. But you won't be needing this speech, because it certainly doesn't explain how to accomplish that, how to think yourself out of a catastrophe. So we'll just keep it and that way you'll have to figure out something else to tell your friends at the MLA. See it as a favor, our contribution to this debate, what do you think?"

I stood up to go. I gathered my belongings. They didn't help me, just watched.

"Anything else?" I asked.

"You didn't answer my question," said the nerdy agent, his glasses twinkling. "About being ambiguous and tentative while you're trying to serve a cause, fighting a war."

"Oh," I said. "Right," I said. "That's the foremost source of tension. Not only for the intellectual, but for every citizen: to battle for what you believe in and yet be critical, be suspicious of your own motives, your own positions, be relentlessly complex. That's the difficulty, always has been. To be transgressive, a pain in the ass, even when the house is burning down."

I turned to go.

Behind me, I heard the voice of the stocky one, the agent who had not even tried to pretend he was remotely interested in one syllable I was pronouncing. "One more thing," that voice said. And I turned again, back towards him. "You know what I think?" he said. "I think you guys are too serious, take yourselves way too seriously. You want people to understand what the hell you're talking about? Try a bit of humor, for a change, what do you say?"

He looked at me as if he were trying to remember my face. I knew I wouldn't forget his.

"I'll think about that," I said. "I'll just have to think about that."

An inevitable postscript:

Everything I recounted above has, obviously, been a gigantic fabrication. Throughout my remarks to the audience at the MLA, I sprinkled numerous clues that I was engaged in a tongue-in-cheek attempt to illustrate the contradictions of intellectual life in our times of turmoil. I referred to Jorge Luis Borges and Vladimir Nabokov, masters of deception and false manuscripts, pushing the absurdity of my tale to inverosimile extremes.

The whole exercise was a gentle way to poke fun at the self importance of intellectuals like myself and my academic public by showing that my high-sounding arguments could not even persuade these two agents, one of whom suggested that I "try a bit of humor" if I wanted to persuade anyone who was not already convinced.

So I followed my own character's advice and told the assembled professors this story.

But I quickly discovered that some took my whimsical literary inventions seriously, way too seriously. One professor later stopped me and wondered why the agents had not Googled my name to determine that I posed no real danger. Another wanted to know if my computer had been confiscated. Still others asked if "those brutes" had roughed me up. A former student of mine told me she was writing a letter to the Washington Post to protest my mistreatment. In an afternoon session, a graduate student confessed to me that my story had filled her with fear because if someone like me could be detained and interrogated, what might happen to ordinary people like her when they enter the United States?

It then dawned on me how deeply my fictional account of detention by Homeland Security agents had resonated with the unbridled fantasies seething inside the heads of so many of my colleagues. I doubted that any of them were about to be sent to Guantanamo Bay, Cuba. And as my spurious agents had pointed out when I tried to convince them that the U.S. is on the verge of becoming a police state, I was free to say anything I wanted at the Modern Language Association convention.

Yet there was no denying that my tale had tapped into a deep paranoia. If entirely rational men and women, experts in literary interpretation and ironical readings, believed me, it was because they must have already imagined the possibility of my sham experience befalling them. Not one of my friends and associates at the convention or afterward dismissed my tall tale as patently absurd. When I lamented the naiveté of my sophisticated audience, the response was unanimous: it was I who was naive.

Maybe they were right. My fraudulent yarn was apparently all too terrifyingly plausible in a country where citizens can be held indefinitely without charges, where domestic overseas telephone calls are monitored by an agency of the government without warrants, where a vice president defends the use of torture against alleged terrorists and where a president invades another country under false pretenses.

The sad truth about my story is that it comes straight out of the trepidation and terror caused by 9/11 and its aftermath that we are still living and that has led to a strongman like Trump being elected. Before that day, I would not even have thought of concocting it, because most Americans would not have understood what I was talking about. The joke would have fallen flat.

The sadder truth is that I can imagine an epilogue to my story.

The United States is hit by an even more lethal terrorist attack.

On that day, can I confidently say that there will not be a knock at my door and that two men, one tall and gangly, the other short and beefy, will not ask me if I recall spreading lies about their efforts to fight the war on terrorism? And that they will not demand that I accompany them, just for a few hours, for some routine questioning?

19.

ALICE IN LEFTLAND:
WILL YOU, WON'T YOU DANCE?[1]

"Tut, tut, child!" said the Duchess. "Everything's got a moral, if only you can find it." —Alice in Wonderland.

Not far from where *Alice's Adventures in Wonderland* was first published in July of 1865 and not many months after the book appeared, a young girl was avidly reading it at the feet of her father as he worked in his London study on an entirely different sort of book, one that would change the world. The daughter's given name was Eleanor but she was known as Tussy in the family. Her father was none other than Karl Marx and he was laboring on *Das Kapital* under unfavorable circumstances: in perpetual debt, a queue of creditors hammering at his door, living "solely on the pawnshop" as he confesses to his benefactor Frederic Engels

1 A considerably different version of this essay was first published in *The Nation* magazine as part of the issue/book that commemorated that journal's 150th anniversary.

in a letter at the end of July of that year, perhaps at the very moment that Tussy was reading Lewis Carroll's masterpiece.

Given how much Marx loved his little Eleanor ("Tussy is me," he once announced), we shouldn't be surprised if the man who inspired most of the major revolutions of the next one hundred and fifty years had read the children's classic that so enthralled her. As to the men and women who led and participated and often suffered in those upheavals, there is also a strong probability that many of them enjoyed Alice, which was, after all, extraordinarily popular (second only, it is said, to Shakespeare and the Bible). More's the pity that most of the radicals and revolutionaries of the next century and a half did not heed some of the lessons hidden in that book that would have abetted them in their quest for justice and peace and freedom, intuitions and gems that might have helped them avoid so many pitfalls and mistakes and defeats, that could have warned them to refuse invitations to multiple Mad Tea Parties that led to disaster instead of paradise.

"The game was in such confusion that she never
knew whether it was her turn or not."

I had read Lewis Carroll's book many times—as a child and then to my own boys and recently with my wife Angélica, simply to relish its chaotic wit—but to once again plunge down the rabbit hole, employing as a lens the perspective of a hundred and fifty years of struggle for a better world, was surprisingly revelatory and frequently disturbing, with sundry phrases and situations resonating with my own experience of progressive activism and engagement over the course of more than five decades.

Had I not spent, along with so many of my luminous comrades, countless hours "busily painting [white roses] red?" Have we not habitually exclaimed to those who would like to sit at our table. "No room! No room!", when there was, in fact, "plenty of room"? And doesn't this sound sadly familiar?: "The players all played at once without waiting for turns, quarrelling all the while, and fighting." Reminiscing about immeasurable meetings with militants of an array of left wing organizations and factions that were, like the mouse, "so easily offended"; having ardently bickered over tiny, rarefied details and abstruse, murky theories, I can't ignore Alice's observation that "the Hatter's remark seemed . . . to have no sort of meaning, and yet it was certainly English." And I found it all-too-easy to identify with Alice as she muses: "It's really dreadful . . . the way all the creatures argue. It's enough to drive one crazy."

To those who nod their heads in appreciation, remembering their own misadventures in Jargonland, Lewis Carroll won't let us off the hook so easily. When Alice, polite and invariably reasonable, presumes—as we would—to be above the surrounding bedlam, the Cheshire Cat has no trouble in proving that she is just as insane as everyone else: "You must be mad," the Cat states irrefutably, "Or you wouldn't have come here."

At times that general madness takes the form of harmless nonsense but it is also often embodied insistently, nightmarishly, in Wonderland violence. "Sentence first," the Queen of Hearts commands, as if she were Stalin or Mao, "verdict afterwards." Beatings, mock trials, threats of imminent execution, inhumane treatment of underlings, and, above all, the incessant chopping off of people's heads at the slightest mistake: "They're dreadfully fond of beheading people here; the great wonder is, that there's anyone left alive!" As if Lewis Carroll were unwittingly warning readers of the looming dangers of dictatorship, whether perpetrated by twentieth century revolutionaries assaulting heaven in the name of the people or regimes trying to salvage capitalism and privilege against the assault by those same neglected, beleaguered people. The crazed rush towards the future justified by the urgency of now, the certainty that "there was not a moment to be lost," so we repeatedly find ourselves impulsively going down the nearest rabbit hole, "never once considering how in the world…to get out again."

> *"Would you tell me, please, which way I ought to walk from here?"*
>
> *"That depends a good deal on where you want to get to," said the Cat.*

So, where do I hope to get to myself with this somber meditation on Alice and her potential adventures in Leftland? Is it fair to turn a book so rowdy and light-hearted into an ominous critique of radical projects and methods? In despondently imitating the gloomy March Hare by selecting only lamentations as my bread and butter, am I not ignoring what is essential, enduring, lovable, emancipating about Lewis Carroll's story and characters?

Because *Alice in Wonderland* can also be read as a seditious text, overflowing with utopian impulses. Why not emphasize Alice's realization "that very few things indeed were really impossible," a credo that has fueled the fire of so many social crusades, that the gay rights movement and the ecological wave of initiatives and protests have recently revealed to be true? Why not blaze in bold letters the words of the Duchess, "The more there is of mine, the less there is of yours"—a dictum that skewers corporations and gluttonous executives who collect millionaire bonuses while rejecting a raise in the minimum wage? The book celebrates rebellion and disobedience (the cook throws frying pans at the Duchess, the Duchess boxes the Queen's ears, the Knave steals tarts, Alice refuses to cooperate, the guinea-pigs cheer despite being suppressed), while despotic figures are derided as bumbling and ineffective.

What we should rescue, above all, from *Alice in Wonderland* is its subversive, rambunctious humor, the same wildness, the same core questioning of authority that has inspired the insurrection and resistance and dissidence of millions over the last century and a half, the imagining of a possible parallel reality that does not obey the rules of a society in dire need of transformation. It is this carnavalesque energy and playfulness that we should recognize and embrace as ours, a crucial part of our progressive identity.

There is a tendency, of course, towards the opposite language and style and demeanor on the left: a heavy, ponderous solemnity, as if all the tragedies of history were weighing us down. We take ourselves, and our discourse, seriously, and for good reason. The suffering is immense, the injustice intolerable, the stupidity widespread, the pillages of the industrial-military-surveillance complex expanding, the future dark and dystopian, the planet on the verge of meltdown.

All the more reason, then, to exult in our own liberation when we have the chance, to revel in the thrill of breaking conventions and interrogating our own beliefs, certitudes and dogmas. All the more reason to recognize the re-enchantment that is reborn with each small act of hope and solidarity, and to extol the sheer joy that accompanies the certainty that we need not leave the world as we found it.

> *"It must be a very pretty dance," said Alice timidly.*
> *"Would you like to see a little of it?" said the Mock Turtle.*
> *"Very much indeed," said Alice.*

During the Chilean Revolution (1970-73), the people of my country marched endlessly, attending interminable rallies in defense of the democratically elected government of Salvador Allende. The energy of those brothers and sisters by my side, their resilience and fortitude and inventiveness, their irrepressible jokes and home-made placards, have inspired me ever since.

What has also stayed with me is how much more vibrant and creative were those men and women in the streets of our cities than most of the men (they were predominantly male) who droned away for hours on the podium, exhorting, analyzing, swearing that the masses could not be stopped. I wondered then, as I do now, so many decades later, why the enthusiasm and defiance of those democratic multitudes was not unleashed, why there was such a contrast between the leaders and the people? And it pains me that our peaceful revolution culminated in a cataclysm, Allende dead, so many tortured, persecuted, exiled, so many dreams that ended, seemed to end.

The King in *Alice in Wonderland* has some grave and presumably commonsensical advice for the White Rabbit about how to tell a story: "Begin at the beginning . . . and go on till you come to the end: then stop."

He is mistaken.

Those of us who thirst for a different world, who seek alternative horizons, know that you do not stop when the end has been reached, that there is no end to our need for justice, that rebels never go "out altogether, like a candle." Rather, we are like the Cheshire Cat. Even when our body has vanished, a grin will always remain obdurately behind, a ghostly presence, to prove that we were once here and may re-emerge, that we can't go on but, as Lewis Carroll's heir, Samuel Beckett, understood, we must go on.

Ultimately, as those of us who still believe in radical change as the only answer to the continuing wars and greed of our suicidal times, this is what we should learn and cherish from *Alice in Wonderland* for the next one hundred and fifty years of illumination and struggle, the challenge that this fantastically absurd text provides us.

After so many tribulations and trials—those we have been through and those that await us anew—are we brave enough to again and again respond to the Mock Turtle's summons: "Will you, won't you, will you, won't you, will you join the dance?"

I believe he is not wrong, that Mock Turtle, when he sings, when he promises as he dances that "there is another shore, you know, upon the other side."

20.

THEY'RE WATCHING US:
SO WHAT?

A FEW YEARS AGO, BEFORE TRUMP WAS EVEN A BLIP ON MY mind, I attended a forum in New York, convened by American PEN, the ACLU, and the Center for National Security at the Fordham School of Law, in order to address the contemporary dilemma of proliferating surveillance in the digital age. During this day experts and participants explored how free expression might exactly be hurt by the new technologies, how spying concretely impacts creative freedom in democratic societies, and tried to come up with ways in which advocacy groups could press the case in Congress and the courts that such an assault on privacy is detrimental to our public discourse and civil liberties.

The forum was entitled, "Surveillance: What's the Harm?", and when it was my turn to speak, I observed that the very question would be greeted with incredulity and more than a tremor of recollected fear if it were posed in my own country, Chile, one of so many unfortunate lands around the world where the legacy of broken bodies and twisted minds, the lingering aftershock of executions and torture, the long term effects of atrocities and persecution and censorship are more than sufficient evidence of the damage a surveillance state can inflict on its populace. For seventeen years—from 1973 to 1990—Chileans suffered a government that expended immense funds and manpower to implement a strategy of terror based on its ability to track down any and all of its citizens and mercilessly punish the slightest hint of misbehavior or rebellious expression.

In my own case, having lived clandestinely in Chile during the first months of the Pinochet dictatorship, I can bear witness to the dread of what it means to be hunted down, praying that those in power do not know your identity, who are your friends or where in the city you happen to be. Soon, however, as my life was in peril, I was ordered by the Resistance to go into exile and thus, with my wife Angélica and our small son, spent the next ten years abroad in the relative freedom of Europe and the United States, dedicated to telling the world the sad story of our land, and the more encouraging one of peaceful insurrection and possible victory.

All this changed when, in 1983, the dictatorship allowed me to return to Santiago.

I found a country drastically changed from the one we had left ten years earlier. People had learned to suspect everyone and anything. Friends who had been outgoing and clear-throated were now hushed and guarded, coding and encrypting each sentence with double and triple entendres. Though the opposition to the regime of General Augusto Pinochet had grown, slowly and painfully reconquering the surface of the country, inching bravely into the public spaces and non-governmental institutions and associations, even the most heroic opponents of the regime, those who risked conspicuousness and defied the authorities, even those protagonists of courage acted with circumspection and detachment, holding back information, avoiding openness, aware that the slightest slip of the tongue could bring down upon them the full force of the secret police.

Upon that first return to Chile in 1983, it was not easy for me, as a writer, to adjust to this culture of shadows and subterfuge, nor to the poisoning and derangement of everyday language. When I spoke, I was told that "Usted no habla en chileno," that I wasn't speaking "in Chilean" or as Chileans now did. Meaning that Chile, the land of Neruda, had become for them synonymous of silence. Meaning that my compatriots felt I did not really recognize what they had been through, that my absence had turned me into an alien, foreign to the culture and the community.

They were right. I was deliberately expressing myself in Chile as I had when I was abroad, trying to preserve the freedom and confidence of a voice diligently cultivated in banishment, almost as if I already inhabited a post-atrocity society. The dictatorship could watch me all it wanted! I had arranged for my own exposure to other eyes—international eyes, powerful eyes—as a way of safeguarding my words: on that 1983 return to Chile, a CBS news crew followed me around; the BBC was interviewing me;

and my *New York Times* editor, Howard Goldberg, had commissioned an op-ed from Santiago.

Presumably protected by the aura of the US and world media, I therefore believed myself to be untouchable, someone too notorious for the generals to maltreat, an arrogance I continued to feel as I phoned in that opinion piece accusing Pinochet of the devastation, misery, and dismay plaguing the land. And I felt even safer once I had finished my dictation; my incendiary words were no longer here in repressive Santiago but way over there in the glorious and sheltered *New York Times* copy center.

But due to a glitch in the recording system, I was forced to dictate the op-ed all over again. Except that this time, I felt completely vulnerable. I was sweating over each provocative statement, certain that the Chilean Gestapo was taking note of every word and would soon cut the phone line, intercept my op-ed so it never reached New York, subvert the protection I had supposedly arranged, and then come and arrest me and my family. During the ten or fifteen minute interval it took to reiterate my prolonged affront to Pinochet, I became aware—truly, scathingly aware—what it meant to be submerged in an atmosphere of unrelenting oppression, exposed and naked for an all-seeing, all-hearing, all-killing tormentor. I understood in my flesh and my skin and my sex why people in my country were exquisitely, brutally careful with what they said and thought and breathed. My ten years of exile and freedom under an inaccessible democratic flag were wiped away, made irrelevant. I became a chileno once again. Somebody malignant and unstoppable was coming for me and my loved ones, they were coming, and there was nowhere to hide, there was no one who could save us.

That initial panic attack lasted for many hours. As it subsided, my very prudent and fearless wife convinced me that my reaction had been irrational. The government couldn't possibly be that much in control, listening to every conversation, pinpointing each subversive statement, monitoring all contacts and intersections. It couldn't possibly translate my English into Spanish instantaneously and act on that information; it couldn't possibly discern my location, find me if I wanted to go underground, detect all the acquaintances whom I had ever crossed paths with. It couldn't predict what I would do. No government could know that much about me.

But perhaps it could.

Many years later, I discovered how overwhelming and pervasive the invasion of privacy in Chile under Pinochet's regime of terror really was. While filming *A Promise to the Dead* in 2006, a documentary by the Canadian director Peter Raymont about my life, we visited the Fundación Salvador Allende and discovered that in its previous incarnation the house where the Fundación was now lodged had been the headquarters of one of the dictatorship's surveillance centers. My host, an old friend from college days, led me to the basement where a tangled snarl of wires were splayed in a multitude of bright colors, coiling in and around each other, listening devices snaking like intertwined vines, left behind on purpose by the former spies to perversely parade a message of impunity, so that whoever descended into that underground cavern would be sickened, as I was, by the sight.

Why did that mesh of twisting wires fill me with such horror? Not only because I realized that my voice and words had been captured there, minutely examined by primitive computers, soiled by the eyes and ears of torturers and executioners; not only because the life of my friends and family, of my beloved Angélica, had been dissected and measured and clicked and scratched to see if pain could be inflicted and secrets excavated; not only because the plural voices of a whole country were squeezed and suffocated inside those cables. But also because that sculpture of foreboding brought into visibility what the government preferred to keep covert, preferred to deny. We all knew that wires like those were buried somewhere: we knew that we were being spied on. That was the point of terror, to let our imagination conjure up and exaggerate the supremacy of those in power. At the same time, in order not to be paralyzed with dread, we had to dismiss that omnipotence, pretend that we could outwit the authorities, picture arenas, no matter how small, of potential liberty, immune from surveillance. It was a mirage, but one that allowed us to remain sane, just as inhabitants of a land beset by earthquakes or tsunamis do not deplete every instant of their days fretting about the next oncoming calamity.

What nauseated me about that warped jungle of bright filaments was how it confirmed our worst suspicions from the past, made me see, really see, the flaunting extent of that interference in our lives, awoke me to the danger we had been in, and suggested this danger was permanent, not merely remote, belonging to faraway yesterdays. Who was to guarantee that someday, someone might not activate a network like this one all over again? Someday? Someone? Why not right then and there, in democratic, supposedly post-atrocity Santiago in 2006? Were not similar links and nexuses and connections and eyes and ears doing the same job, eavesdropping, collecting data and voices and knowledge for a day when the men in the shadows might be asked to once again intervene drastically in our lives?

And why only in Santiago? What about America today where, compared to the data-crunching clout of the NSA and other dis-intelligence agencies, Pinochet's multi-colored wires look puny and outdated, like a samurai sword compared to the airman above, in the Enola Gay, about to drop a nuclear bomb on Hiroshima? What about elsewhere on this planet where democratic governments far and wide systematically spy on their own citizens? Aren't we all in harm's way? And now that a paranoid maniac like Trump is President and Jeff Sessions is his Attorney General and "the shackles are off," as Sean Spicer so eloquently put it, hasn't the danger become far greater?

Most people living in the United Sates and other countries subject to the rule of law would still respond by taking comfort in the distance between a dictatorship like Chile and the sort of open society that they inhabit. And rightly so. It was heartening that revelations about NSA illegal snooping and over-reach were originally met by a massive critical reaction in the press, in Congress and, of course, abroad, where the indignation of German, French, Brazilian, Mexican and Spanish leaders led—or so we have been told, who knows with what degree of truth—to significant changes in the way the United States would authorize eavesdropping, at least for "allies." Of course, the U.S. government will continue to spy, even more so now, in this dismal and increasingly authoritarian 2017 no matter what limited and cosmetic restrictions, if any, may henceforth be enacted, and of course the process of criminalization of journalists who question or inform about these activities and methods is bound to increase as leaks and whistleblowers inevitably proliferate, worse than ever given Trump's belief that the press is the enemy of the people and that any criticism is fake news. But, again, ordinary citizens can derive some solace from the fact that they are at least not threatened with the arbitrary repression and onslaught that we suffered in Chile merely because we wanted to exercise our right to speak freely and think divergently. And yet, almost every time I bring up the cautionary example of Chile, I tend to be harangued with something approaching flippancy: hey, not to worry, what happened there can't happen here.

A warning for those who bask in the glow of that self-congratulatory phrase, "It can't happen here." We also chanted those words in the streets of Santiago and from the hills of Valparaíso before the coup swept our lives away. We also labored under the delusion that our oh-so-stable democracy was exempt from the savagery of history and the ravages of an unbridled government. We also were targeted by a regime that defined dissidents as terrorists. We also consented to the degradation of our speech.

And we have also realized that, of the many crimes tyrants commit against their own people, the most persistent and enduring crime of all may be the one committed against language. Even today in Chile, more than twenty years after we reconquered democracy and seven years after the death of Pinochet, most people there are still wary of using the word dictatorship to refer to the past, preferring the more neutral "régimen militar." I could multiply examples of this toxic avoidance of significance and, therefore, of reality. Instead of "torture," for instance, we have "excesses." Instead of "crimes," we have "mistakes." Instead of "golpe militar" we are tendered "pronunciamiento," as if this had been a matter of words pronounced rather than virulence delivered. "Golpe" is a violent blow; pronunciamiento means that the soldiers have given vent to an idea, the need to change the government.

Behind the destruction of language lurks the destruction of trust in one another. We also watched how so many of our countrymen, fearful for their safety, looked away as human rights were violated, and today continue to bear the toxic burden of guilt for not having protested, for not having defended those unjustly accused and victimized.

Surveillance, in any land where it is ubiquitous and inescapable, generates distrust and divisions among its citizens and their readiness to speak freely to each other diminishes their willingness to even dare to think freely.

It can always happen here. It can happen anywhere.

Look at the internment of the Japanese-Americans during

World War II. Look at McCarthyism and the red scare. Look at the subsequent decades of self-censorship that still persist. Or go back to the Espionage Act of 1917 and the 1918 Sedition Act. Or plumb the origins of the Republic and the Alien and Sedition Act of 1798.

But why journey so far into the past?

As the 2001 Patriot Act proves (only 66 members of the House and one member of the Senate voted against it), if people are frightened enough, manipulated enough, fear-mongered enough, they are more than willing to abrogate their own freedom, as so many did in Chile, in the name of personal and national security. And if there were to be another terrorist attack like the vile ones perpetrated on September 11th 2001, even more invasive surveillance would be eagerly authorized, indeed demanded. Think of what fanatics like them could do with such colossal executive muscle at their disposal. Though what's unsettling is to grasp that prospective tyrants wouldn't require new legislation, now as during so much American history, to rein in free expression.

Because now, right now, there is in place a state surveillance system that already can pry into every aspect of our lives. At this very moment, anonymous and unelected administrators scoop up and store megadata that has the potential to allow them or their masters to manipulate, blackmail, influence, browbeat, hound their fellow citizens into submission.

What is most dismaying about this situation—and most astounding to someone from a country where activists and intellectuals were able to survive because we were cunning enough to hide our secrets and thwart the spying—is that most of the records available about our lives in contemporary society does not come from a furtive government program. They are incessantly culled and mined from consensual exchange, happily, voluntarily, loudly offered up to the blatant gods of commerce and the Internet. The same people who fume about totalitarian meddling in their existence seem to be blissfully unaware that digital eyeballs are measuring and bundling and gouging their every action, every hit, every profile, every purchase, every trip, every medicine, every texting, every friending, every like, every smile, every frown.

What a contrast with Chileans who, when under the boot, were vibrantly aware of the damage to our body and souls if we were not cautious when we communicated. Hoping to become invisible, to disappear so that we would not be "disappeared," taken away and never heard of again. Lucky for us that in Pinochet's time we had no Facebook or Twitter, no Instagram or Tumblr or MapQuesting, no linked grid of consumer signals that would have been more efficient than any intelligence agency in tracking down our mysteries and passions and preferences. Lucky for us that we were not subjected to logarithms gone berserk, Googled or Amazoned or iPhoned into overtness and disclosure, lucky for us that our secret police could not use these instruments to predict with remarkable accuracy our acquaintances, our desires, our obscurities, our whereabouts. Or perhaps we would have been smart enough or scared enough back then to withdraw from those social media networks and live, hermit-like, in the wastelands of existence, removed from the everyday Web of ordinary human events.

Or would we? Would the majority of the people who resisted the dictatorship have been able to extricate themselves from the daily desires and temptations of the mini-celebrity, attention-seeking society, the credit cards and iPads and cellphones that are as prevalent in Chile today as they are in the United States and the rest of the planet? Post-atrocity Chileans, like so many other inhabitants of lands across the globe who have lived through dictatorships and transitioned to precarious democracies, uneasily participate in both worlds, the traumatic one they have left behind and the consumer world they are shopping and texting in now. Inside their minds prowl the harrowing memories of distress carried out in attics and dark cellars that still erode the public trust; while outside they celebrate the falsely sunny consumer universe of exposure and display that creates an excess of trust. Would we, can we, do we even wish to, escape the social media universe of our time?

In *The Circle*, his best-selling novel that is now a film, Dave Eggers paints a disquieting answer to that question. In the dystopian world of the Circle, where all human activity is under the constant and cheerful surveillance of an omniscient and godlike mega-corporation, social media users gladly give up their liberty and privacy, invariably for the most benevolent of platitudes and reasons. Arguing that such overweening power accumulated in such few hands would never be allowed in democratic societies misses the point. What is chilling about *The Circle* is how willingly the protagonist, Mae Holland, submits to the dictates requiring absolute and instantaneous transparency in all human affairs, how needy she is, how typical, how representative, how unaware she is of the perils embedded in her desire to belong, to believe, to succumb. Instead of answering "yes" to questions posed by her minders, Mae answers, over and over again, I do, I do, I do, subconsciously implying that she has become the spiritual bride of the smiling Frankenstein of the world wide web.

She barely realizes the harm being done to her humanity.

Is this the future?

Possibly. Literature often helps us discern the hidden currents contained in the present, portending what may come to pass.

Let me respond to some of the apprehensions I have been expressing in this essay with my own prophetic piece of literature.

During one of my many returns to dictatorial Chile, I wrote a fable for children entitled *La Rebelión de los Conejos Mágicos, The Rabbits' Rebellion.*

In that story, the King of the Wolves invades the land of the rabbits and immediately decrees that rabbits do not exist. He expunges them from books and bans their name from being mentioned privately or publicly. He sets up a gigantic system of pythons that slither through houses and hawks that fly everywhere, insuring that nobody contravene his commands. Still, in order to dispel persistent rumors that the bunnies are audaciously alive, he orders a series of photos of himself taken by a monkey photographer, whose daughter happens to be a big fan of the rabbits and insists, in spite of being punished by her parents, that the forbidden creatures come to visit her in dreams. The photographer soon finds himself in trouble, because each photo that he takes and is displayed all over the kingdom so the Wolf's eyes can scrutinize all actions of his citizens, each and every photo ends up being infiltrated and overrun, timidly at first, and then more daringly, by the recalcitrant rabbits. No matter how much the photographer and the Wolf-King's counselors try to erase their presence, the mischievous ears of the rabbits keep intruding into the margins of the photo. And when his Wolfiness erects a gigantic throne to prove that he is invulnerable, the rabbits finally decide to move out of the photos and into reality, munching away at the legs of the throne until it comes crashing down. The final directive of the Wolf-King before he retreats into anonymity is to the photographer: don't print this picture!

But those are not the last words of the story. The last words belong to the little monkey girl who would not let her imagination be subdued, who kept dreaming of rebellion despite the fear and spying that reigned in that kingdom. I trust that the last words of that children's story written decades ago during a brutal dictatorship, still resonate today.

The world, the story says—the world, the story predicts—the world is and was and will be full of rabbits.

21.

HOW WE OVERCAME TYRANNY BEFORE: TAKE HEART, FRIENDS

FROM MY HOME, HERE IN SANTIAGO DE CHILE, I LOOK UP AT the immense mountain range of the Andes and my spirits are lifted. Since my childhood, these mountains have bestowed on me a sense of security and permanence sadly absent from my life, but in these troubling times, they afford me something else: an intimation of hope.

Because, exactly 200 years ago, on Feb. 12, 1817, a group of men crossed these very Andes, impenetrable, colossal, majestic, in an extraordinary journey that was to liberate Chile from colonial rule. Their exploits became a turning point in the emancipation of all Spanish-speaking America.

Starting in 1810, across the continent, patriots stirred by the European Enlightenment and encouraged by the successful revolt of the 13 American colonies against their British masters had worked to cast off the imperial yoke of Spain. From Mexico to the Southern Cone, independence movements introduced an array of reforms that make Latin Americans proud to this day.

In Chile, in particular, freedom was the watchword: freedom of the press and freedom to assemble, freedom to elect our own representatives to a National Congress, freedom to trade with any nation and freedom to receive a secular education beyond the stifling reach of the church. And most crucially, my country adopted Libertad de Vientres, the Freedom of Wombs law, which established that any child born of a slave was immediately free.

In spite of these achievements, those first years of Chile's independence were fraught. Fratricidal conflict between moderates and radicals weakened the cause of reform. By 1814, the Spanish crown had reconquered many of the mutinous territories it had lost, a period known, precisely, as La Reconquista.

In October that year, after defeat at the battle of Rancagua, near Santiago, the remaining contingent of the patriotic army retreated across the Andes to the province of Mendoza, in Argentina, one of the few lands that remained in the hands of the revolutionaries. From there, as they plotted their return, they had to watch the restored Spanish overlords annul the independence movement's liberal transformations. A Tribunal of Vigilance and Public Security set up a reign of terror—torture, jailings, executions, deportations, expropriations—to curb defiance.

A century and a half later, in 1973, a tyrannical regime of violence visited Chile once more in the name of conservative values and oligarchical interests. The dictatorship of Gen. Augusto Pinochet not only attacked the left-wing reforms of Salvador Allende, but also systematically erased advances in social and civil rights—indeed, the welfare state—for which generations of Chileans had fought since independence.

After the 1973 military takeover, just as in the dark days of La Reconquista, those opponents of the regime who stayed in the country and those who, like myself, my wife and countless others, became exiles were comforted by the example of how, at the dawn of its sovereign history, our country had been liberated by an epic struggle against fear and subjugation.

We would repeat to ourselves the story of the "Ejército Libertador de los Andes," the rugged army of patriots who had crossed the same cordillera I contemplate as I write these words. Thousands of troops (many of them former slaves), mules and horses, dozens of scouts and some scores of civilians, including auxiliary and medical personnel, took a perilous route.

The Argentine general José de San Martín and the Chilean leader Bernardo O'Higgins, both revered as founding fathers of their respective republics, were bold and inventive enough to believe that the Andes would be not a barrier to their search for justice, but a friend. Though hungry, thirsty and exhausted, the insurgents beat the Spanish forces of La Reconquista on Feb. 12, 1817, at the battle of Chacabuco.

Inspired by that distant feat, 20th-century Chileans also found the strength, patience, craftiness and unity to vanquish their oppressor, the Pinochet dictatorship. We did so by occupying every space possible, invading every corner and organization of the country, unshackling our fetters one by one. It took 17 painful years, and many dead and disappeared, but today we enjoy a thriving democracy that is constantly seeking to expand the rights of all people—men, women, immigrants, students, pensioners, workers, artists.

Would that I could say the same of the world at large.

All over the globe, the slow but steady accomplishments of the past are under siege. Worse still, the earth itself is threatened by climate disaster and extinction. The forces of regression and authoritarianism, contemporary avatars of La Reconquista, are on the march in country after country, fueled by ethnic nationalism. Walls are going up along borders as swiftly as the hearts of millions are closing to solidarity. Rights that we had considered unassailable and secure are being eroded.

Not since the iniquity of Hitler and Mussolini have we witnessed such a resurgence of hatred against the Other, even as the United States—one of the countries that led the fight against fascism—is now governed by men who would turn back the clock, and use repression rather than persuasion to obliterate so many gains and glories we took for granted.

Having seen in my own country how easily a proud democracy can be replaced by the most terrifying of tyrannies, I believe it is never too soon to issue a warning about the dangers ahead. If I invoke, 200 years later, the example of those revolutionary patriots who were undeterred in their quest for liberty by catastrophic odds and some of the highest mountains on the planet, it is not because I think that an invasion from abroad is the answer to the daunting challenges humanity faces. It is for what we can learn today about resistance and hope from the Army of the Andes.

Just as those fighters for independence found a sanctuary from which to gather strength, so should the multitudes who struggle now for justice and equality seek a similar haven. From that place of safety, we can hold firm against the forces of fear and reaction, and inch by inch, take back our land—bold in the knowledge that no obstacle is too large, no enemy too mighty, no mountain range of desolation and death too insurmountable.

Each of us occupies some space of respite from the whirlwind, each of us has something to contribute, our own Andes to cross, if we are to prevail. The mountains of Chile tell us that if we are brave enough, resourceful enough, imaginative enough, then nothing in this miraculous world is impossible.

22.

THE WHISPERING LEAVES OF THE
HIROSHIMA GINGKO TREES

O N AUG. 6, 1945, A 14-YEAR-OLD SCHOOLBOY NAMED AKIHIRO Takahashi was knocked unconscious by a deafening roar and flash of blinding light. When he awoke, he found he had been thrown many yards by the detonation of the atom bomb dropped on Hiroshima. He had survived because his school was about a mile from the epicenter of the blast.

Dazed and burned, Akihiro headed to the river to cool himself. Along the way, he witnessed a scene of apocalypse: corpses strewn like rocks, a baby crying in the arms of its charred mother, scalded men peppered with shards of glass, their clothes melted, wandering like ghosts through the wasteland, the unbreathable darkened air, the raging conflagrations. In an instant, about 85,000 men, women and children had perished. In the days and months that followed, tens of thousands more slowly succumbed to their injuries and the effects of radiation.

I met Akihiro Takahashi in 1984, when he was the director

of the Hiroshima Peace Memorial Museum. By then middle-aged, his body was a testament to that war crime and its aftermath. One ear was flat and mangled, his hands were gnarled and from a finger on each grew a black fingernail.

"You must see the Hibakujumoku, the survivor trees," he said to me, almost as an order, at the end of a long conversation in his office. "You must see the gingkos."

It was the first time I had ever heard of this tree. With one of his twisted hands, he gestured toward the city beyond the museum. They were a sign of wonder, the three trees that I visited, in the Hosen-Ji and Miyojoin-Ji temples and at the Shukkeien gardens, spreading and magnificent and resilient.

The gingko, I learned, was an expert in survival, a species found in fossils 270 million years old. These specific trees had been saved because their roots underground had been spared the nuclear annihilation. Within days of the explosion they had sprouted new greenery surrounded though they were by Hiroshima's horrors of carbonized bodies and black rain and wailing survivors.

The gingkos, Akihiro Takahashi said, expressed better than anything he could say through an interpreter the endurance of hope, the need for peace and reconciliation.

And so, decades later, when the majestic old oak trees in front of our home in the United States were rotting and had to be cut down, it seemed natural to us to replace them with gingko trees. We purchased two specimens, and paid to have them planted along the street we live on, and we convinced the city forestry department to plant a third nearby.

The choice was not simply a challenge to death — though these trees would live far beyond the limits of the oaks, and would be here when we were long gone — but also an aesthetic decision. The gingkos are elegant and supple, their leaves are delicate lobes of green shaped like tiny fans.

I watered these miraculous trees every day and greeted them each morning. On occasion, I even spoke and sang to them.

I thought of Akihiro Takahashi again the other day. Early one morning, my wife and I woke to discover a crew of workers excavating huge holes right next to the roots of our gingko trees in order to make room for thick coils of snaking yellow tubes of fiber-optic cables. As soon as I saw what was happening, I sprang into action. It helped that I could speak Spanish to the workers. I argued vehemently   and persuaded them to dig their trenches farther from the gingkos' roots. I checked to see that other trees in the street were unharmed and then went home to fire off emails to the city authorities to ensure that inspectors oversaw future encroachments of this sort.

Though our particular trees are safe, I am haunted by deeper, more ominous thoughts about how this great survivor now seems threatened by the depredations of modernity: the gingko vs. the gigabyte. This is, after all, a conflict between nature in its most pristine, slow and sublime form and the demands of a high-speed society that, armed with an astonishing technological prowess, wants to expand everywhere, burrow through any obstacle in its way, communicate instantly with infinite efficiency. The battle is one the Earth is losing as this Sixth Extinction, a manmade extinction, wreaks its havoc on land, water and air, on our plants and creatures.

I am far from being a Luddite. In this isolationist, chauvinistic era, I welcome the human connections that our global communications networks enable. They at least offer a glimmer of what we might achieve, the peace and understanding between different cultures and nations that Mr. Takahashi dreamt of, all those years ago in Hiroshima. Yet, as we heedlessly rush into the future with our arrogant machinery, will we ever stop to ponder the consequences? How many species are threatened today by our insatiable desires, our incessant overdevelopment, our inability to measure joy and happiness by anything other than by the latest gadget?

The Hiroshima gingkos, the tenacious older brothers and sisters of the tender green trees in front of our North Carolina house, were able to resist the most devastating outcome of science and technology, the splitting of the atom, a destructive power that could turn the whole planet into rubble. Those trees' survival was a message of hope in the midst of the black rain of despair: that we could nurture life and conserve it, that we must be wary of the forces we unleash.

How paradoxical, how sad, how stupid, it would be if, more than seven decades after Hiroshima opened the door to the possible suicide of humanity, we did not understand that warning from the past, that call to the future, what the gentle leaves of the gingko trees are still trying to tell us.

A NOTE ON THE ESSAYS

The first version of "Grieving for America" appeared in Salon on November 6, 2016, and then, in another, post-election incarnation, on November 9th in *El País* (Madrid), *Página Doce* (Buenos Aires) and *Proceso* (Mexico City) under the title "América se quita la máscara." Other parts of this introduction were written specially for this book.

"Phillip II, the Sixteenth Century Spanish Monarch, Writes to His Excellency Donald Trump" was published in *Time* on March 10, 2016, under the title "The Prudent King's Advice to Trump." This version is slightly longer.

"America Meets Frankenstein" was published in *Time* on September 6th, 2016, under the title "The Case for Feeling Compassion Toward Trump Supporters." This version is slightly longer.

"My Mother and Trump's Border" was published in Salon on September 25, 2016.

A first version of "Latin American Food and the Failure of Trump's Wall" was published in the *Los Angeles Times* on November 4, 2012, under the title "The Other Melting Pot" and has been substantially rewritten for this book.

"Faulkner's Question for America" originally appeared in *The Atlantic* on November 4, 2016, under the title "Will America Earn the Right to Survive?"

"Now, America, You Know How Chile Felt" originally appeared in *The New York Times* on December 16, 2016. Another piece on American intervention in the affairs of foreign countries, akin to this one, was published on the CNN website on July 29, 2016. Not included here, it can be read at http://www. cnn.com/2016/07/29/opinions/hillary-clinton-donald-trump-illegal-electoral-interference-ariel-dorfman/.

A first version of "The River Kwai Passes Through Latin America and the Potomac: What it Feels Like to be Tortured" was published at Tomdispatch on June 17, 2014, in conjunction with *The Nation*, under the title "How to Forgive Your Torturer: The River Kwai Passes Through Latin America and Washington." It has been rewritten and updated for this book.

"Words of Encouragement for Donald Trump from James Buchanan, the Worst President in U.S. History" originally appeared in *The Los Angeles Times* on January 19, 2017.

"A Message from the End of the World" originally appeared in *The New York Times* on March 31, 2017.

"Should Iago Be Tortured?" was originally published in *The New York Times* on July 23, 2017, in a different version titled "Shakespeare's Torture Test."

A different and earlier version of "Mission Akkomplished: From Comrade Bush to Tovarisch Trump" was published in *The New Statesman* on May 8, 2006 with the title "Mission Akkomplished: Mayday for Comrade Bush." It has been drastically rewritten for the Trump era.

"Martin Luther King Marches On" was originally transmitted by the BBC on August 27, 2003, under the title "Martin Luther King: A Latin American Perspective," and published on August 28th, 2003 on Tomdispatch with the title "What Martin Luther King Might Say Today." Tomdispatch then published, on August 27, 2013, an updated and revised version titled "Martin Luther King and the Two 9/11s." The text that appears in this book has been revised yet again for the Trump era.

"Searching for Mandela" is a speech delivered on July 31, 2010, in Johannesburg, originally titled "Whose Memory? Whose Justice?: A Meditation on How and When And If To Reconcile," published on the Mandela Foundation website (https://www.nelsonmandela.org/news/entry/eighth-nelson-mandela-annual-lecture-address) and in several other papers, journals and websites.

"The Truth That Made Her Free" was published in *The New York Times Book Review* on December 23, 2016.

A very different version of "The Dancing Cosmos of Albert Einstein" was published in *The New Statesman* under the title "Dancing To His Tune" on August 29, 2005. It has been considerably updated due to new scientific information and experiments.

"Reading Cervantes in Captivity" is a longer version of a piece in *The New York Times Book Review* on October 9, 2016, titled "In Exile with 'Don Quixote'."

"Revisiting Melville in Chile" was published by *The Nation* on May 10, 2017 under the title "What Hermann Melville Can Teach Us About the Trump Era."

"Homeland Security Ate My Speech" has been drastically rewritten and updated from a version first published in the 2006 edition of *Profession*, the Journal of the Modern Language Association, under the title "The Lost Speech."

"Alice in Leftland: Will You, Won't You Dance?" was commissioned by The Nation for its 150th Anniversary Issue, and published on April 6, 2015 by that magazine with the title "Separated at Birth."

"They're Watching Us: So What?" has been substantially revised from its original version published in *Guernica* on February 3, 2014, titled "Repression By Any Other Name."

"How We Overcame Tyranny Before: Take Heart, Friends" was originally published in *The New York Times* on February 11, 2017.

"The Whispering Leaves of the Hiroshima Gingko Leaves" was originally published in *The New York Times* on August 5, 2017.

ACKNOWLEDGEMENTS

In times of trouble and defeat, we must always be wary of succumbing to a feeling of hopelessness. I have not been immune from the easy enticement of that feeling but also have fortunately had by my side, when things seemed most dismal, the luminous company of those who have saved me from the temptation of despair.

This book would not be possible without that company, the many others who contributed in one way or another so that I did not need to face in solitude the demons inside and outside my life.

None of these pieces would have been published in their current form if not for the attentive, painstaking, re-reading and improving, in English and in Spanish, of multiple drafts, by Angélica, my partner in life and literature, to whom this collection, as everything else I write, is dedicated.

Our friend, my assistant, Suzan Senerchia, provided indispensable support, finding books and articles that helped me compose these comments, which range widely—and often wildly—over an array of materials and interests.

My agents for this volume, Jacqueline Ko and Anna Wood, helped steer it to the right port. They also worked tirelessly, with others at the Wylie Agency, to place the pieces originally in a variety of outlets.

I cannot mention all the editors at each of those venues, but I would like to particularly recognize some of them: Tom Engelhardt at Tomdispatch, Matt Seaton at *The New York Times* op ed page; Parul Sehgal and Gal Beckerman, at *The New York Times Book Review*; Roane Carey and Don Guttenplan at *The Nation*; Cherry Gee and Susan Brenneman at *The Los Angeles Times* op ed page; Pat Wiedenkeller at the opinion section of CNN; diverse editors at *Guernica, Time, The Atlantic*, the BBC, and Salon; and, of course, my editors in Spanish, Ernesto Tieffenberg (*Página Doce*), Rafael Rodríguez Castañeda (*Proceso*), and José Andrés Rojo Ramírez (*El País*).

To my new friends at OR Books, who decided to risk bringing out these writings at an uncertain moment of political crisis and instability, my thanks particularly to John Oakes and Colin Robinson for their belief in my work and its relevance.

Finally, there is the family, those who afford Angélica and me sustenance in a variety of caring ways: Rodrigo, Isabella and Catalina; Joaquín and Cece; Pedro, Ana Maria, and Patricio; Nathalie and Ryan; Heather and her two daughters Kayleigh and Emmy and her parents Sharon and Kirby. And my gratitude as well to friends, too numerous to list here, some so close that we feel them to be family.

Without all of you, I would have been far lonelier in my struggle against the toxic mixture of hatred, ignorance, and prejudice that contaminates us all, and in my ongoing attempts to make sense of what is worst in our species and basest in an America that must indeed be exorcised by its most radiant citizens, like so many loved ones near me, if we are to survive.

O/R C

Desperately Seeking Self-Improvement
A Year Inside the Optimization Movement
CARL CEDERSTRÖM AND ANDRÉ SPICER

Old Demons, New Deities
Twenty-One Short Stories from Tibet
EDITED BY TENZIN DICKIE

Homeland Security Ate My Speech
Messages from the End of the World
ARIEL DORFMAN

Assuming Boycott
Resistance, Agency, and Cultural Production
EDITED BY KAREEM ESTEFAN, CARIN KUONI, AND LAURA RAICOVICH

Divining Desire
Focus Groups and the Culture of Consultation
LIZA FEATHERSTONE

The Spread Mind
Why Consciousness and the World Are One
RICCARDO MANZOTTI

The Candidate
Jeremy Corbyn's Improbable Path to Power
ALEX NUNNS

With Ash on Their Faces
Yezidi Women and the Islamic State
CATHY OTTEN

Ours to Hack and to Own
The Rise of Platform Cooperativism, a New Vision for the Future of Work and a Fairer Internet
EDITED BY TREBOR SCHOLZ AND NATHAN SCHNEIDER

What's Yours Is Mine
Against the Sharing Economy
TOM SLEE